PRAI

Finding Your Way i

and Dr. Sonya Bruton

"*Finding Your Way in the Nonprofit Sector* is a thought-pro-voking and authentic journey from an accomplished, professional, brilliant writer and experienced mentor who makes you feel like you are having an intimate—and honest—conversation with a *friend!* Dr. Bruton provides a framework for achieving the self-understanding required to successfully facilitate fulfillment in the lives of others while *simultaneously* achieving professional and personal satisfaction in one's own life. You won't be able to put this book down as you journey with Dr. B. through the Five *C*s."

—DR. ORLANDO L. TAYLOR

Executive director and Co-PI, Center for the Advancement of STEM Leadership
Immediate past chair, board of directors, Council for Higher Education Accreditation
Distinguished fellow, American Association of Colleges and Universities
Professor and Dean Emeritus, Howard University
Fielding Graduate University

"As someone who has traveled between the for-profit and social service–sector worlds, I find myself wishing I had benefited from this gem of a book way back when. Dr. Sonya Bruton has given us exactly what the subtitle says: a portable mentor, one that reflects the wisdom of a leader who has experienced her own transformative career and now shares those pearls with us."

—GEORGE P. TILSON, EDD

Coauthor, *Working Relationships: Creating Career Opportunities for People with Disabilities Through Business Partnerships*, with foreword by Richard E. Marriott

"At work, we are always in development. In *Finding Your Way in the Nonprofit Sector*, Dr. Sonya Bruton demonstrates practical, effective ways to avoid being overwhelmed and grow into a rewarding career in human services. How far you grow is how far you go. When you and your team grow in an environment of psychological safety, everyone feels more deeply committed to the organization. With stories rooted in real-world challenges she has overcome, Dr. Bruton shares her hard-won experience navigating relationships for collaboration and support and managing managers to foster a culture of learning. This is a master class in nonprofit management to advance your career with meaning and fulfillment. With this portable mentor, you will find *your* way. Readable, actionable, and uplifting."

—JESSICA HARTUNG

Entrepreneur

Author, *The Conscious Professional: Transform Your Life at Work*

"Through her experience and expertise, Dr. Bruton offers advice via a virtual portable mentor for emerging social service leaders, thoughtfully outlining an inquisitive and self-guided approach to cultivating connections, networking, and peer learning."

—TESS KUENNING

President and CEO, Bi-State Primary Care Association

"In *Finding Your Way in the Nonprofit Sector*, Dr. Bruton combines personal experience and empirical evidence to produce a guide that is both educational and specific to the needs of the young professional. This pocket mentor supports young professionals across disciplines in finding their way through tasks that are collaborative, community-based, and rooted in care. The Five Cs eloquently articulate personal and professional tasks to aid young professionals in thriving."

—KYARA A. GREEN, M.S.
Clinical Psychology Doctoral Candidate

"At a time in our world when many are searching for guidance on how to lead and serve with greater purpose, Dr. Bruton's book offers an honest, practical blueprint on how to achieve success in the nonprofit sector. This book navigates through organizational trenches and around leadership landmines to higher levels of awareness. This is a must read!"

—RHONDA G. RANEY
Attorney and Non-Profit Agency Executive, Mediation Solutions

"This is a terrific book. I'd recommend it to just about anyone at any stage trying to find their way in the nonprofit world. Dr. Bruton writes in the spirit of the best mentors. Drawing on her deep well of experience, she offers us a refreshingly clear, candid, and compelling path forward. Finding your way is practical and inspiring. Read it now and come back to it again and again."

—DR. DELLA POLLOCK
Professor Emerita, University of North Carolina at Chapel Hill, Founding Director, Marian Cheek Jackson Center

"Dr. Bruton has very intentionally, and accurately, created answers to many questions one finds oneself asking in many workplace scenarios. This portable mentor is indeed that. It is the handy manual that one keeps referring back to when wondering, "What just happened here?" Dr. Bruton's insight and wisdom looks at the social services sector, but many of her examples and solutions are extremely helpful in almost any work environment. I look forward to suggesting this work to upcoming graduates as well as seasoned workplace vets who could benefit from her wise counsel and action step questions."

—MICHELLE HAMMOND

Associate Vice President for the Library and Learning Commons at Goucher College

Finding Your Way
in the Nonprofit Sector

Your Portable Mentor
for Avoiding Pitfalls
and Seizing Opportunities

DR. SONYA BRUTON

Advantage | Books

Published by Advantage, Charleston, South Carolina.
Member of Advantage Media.

ADVANTAGE is a registered trademark, and the Advantage colophon is a trademark of Advantage Media Group, Inc.

Printed in the United States of America.

10 9 8 7 6 5 4 3 2 1

ISBN: 978-1-64225-412-9 (Paperback)
ISBN: 978-1-64225-414-3 (eBook)

LCCN: 2022919654

Cover design by Danna Steele.
Layout design by Matthew Morse.

This publication is designed to provide accurate and authoritative information in regard to the subject matter covered. It is sold with the understanding that the publisher is not engaged in rendering legal, accounting, or other professional services. If legal advice or other expert assistance is required, the services of a competent professional person should be sought.

Advantage Media helps busy entrepreneurs, CEOs, and leaders write and publish a book to grow their business and become the authority in their field. Advantage authors comprise an exclusive community of industry professionals, idea-makers, and thought leaders. Do you have a book idea or manuscript for consideration? We would love to hear from you at **AdvantageMedia.com**.

To my mother, Patricia T. Jackson, and my grandmothers, Marian C. Jackson and Kuma Lee Thompson, who gave me everything that they had and taught me to return it tenfold. My love of the written word comes from those matriarchs and my dad, Boyd Jackson Jr., who made learning from and loving books cool.

To my son, Kevin D. Bruton, who motivates me to pave the way for him and his generation.

CONTENTS

Why You Should Read This Book

My "why" begins with a personal story that reflects exactly the kind of consequences that can ensue if you enter *any* sector without knowing what you're getting into. It is not a pleasant experience.

My first job out of college was a developmental initiative, sponsored by Knight Ridder newspapers, designed to groom the next generation of publishers. In the "fast track to management" program, I spent six months in each business department covering vacant positions for varying intervals of time. I went from filling in for an outside sales representative on maternity leave for three months to serving as the staff writer in the marketing department for another three months. These rotations amounted to a cross-training initiative on steroids, with one trial by fire after another. I was one of two of the first undergraduate degree holders accepted into the program of otherwise MBA graduates. They placed me in Tallahassee, Florida, one of their smaller markets, believing that a smaller setting would provide a more nurturing environment. It was the opposite.

The reduced staff size meant that everyone knew about my unique work arrangement and the payment that I received. I was placed in Tallahassee, but I was hired by corporate and received wages based on Miami pay scales, which were a little more than double the rates paid in northern Florida. They were also aware that I had no training in business. My degree was in news-editorial journalism. I was trained to write the news, not publish it. That meant that in each department, I was learning every aspect of the operation for the first time. My trainers and coworkers resented the setup. They wanted to know why corporate was investing the money and giving the executive leadership opportunity to new graduates rather than the employees responsible for the company's success. They also assumed it was a minority-focused enterprise, because I am black. It was not.

Their umbrage and my naivete created a perfect storm. I was unprepared for the work and the hostility. I was a fast learner of the tasks that I was being exposed to, but I was completely clueless about office politics and corporate culture. I did not understand the rules of the business game, so I was violating them over and over again and not benefiting from proven assimilation strategies. As a result, I was constantly perplexed by the reactions of others and found myself becoming alienated rather than connected. I needed help.

I reached out to my college advisor, Harry Amana, for assistance. He put me in touch with an organizational psychologist who told me that, in effect, I was derailing myself. She instructed me to read *Games Your Mother Never Taught You: Corporate Gamesmanship for Women* by Betty Harragan to turn things around. I read it, and I followed Harragan's advice.

That book saved my career—and it is why I wrote this book for people who want to succeed in what is often an unfamiliar environment: the social services sector, where making a difference is an essential part of every job.

When I left the newspaper industry in 1993, I entered the social services sector, "that part of social and economic activity done for the purpose of benefiting society and which is funded, in part or whole, through charitable gifts."[1] I found my fit there, and I want to help you find yours.

There are many business books that teach you how to navigate the corporate sector but not nearly enough for the social services domain, which is the landing spot for those searching for meaning. In fact, Goodhire found that 60 percent of millennials and 51 percent of Generation Xers find great meaning and purpose in their work and would opt for careers with meaning and flexibility over those that pay the most.[2] I appreciate this, as it is the need for purpose, impact, meaning, and flexibility that informed my own choices. For that reason, I would like to give to you what was given to me when I entered a foreign environment: a clear and simple road map for orienting yourself to the social services work landscape.

This book will be most beneficial for those who are working in that sector, are about to enter it, or are contemplating entering it, but there is also something here for anyone who cares about doing well in their chosen profession. Many corporations are leaning in to the social enterprise model that blends social-sector values with corporate structures and methods. If you work in a hybrid organization or are in the midst of adapting your culture to better retain and recruit talent that cares about creating a social benefit as well as earning a living,

---

1   Jan Fletcher, "What Is a Social Sector?," SmartCapitalMind, May 28, 2022, https://www.smartcapitalmind.com/what-is-a-social-sector.htm.

2   Sara Korolevich, "The Meaning of Work in 2021 — A Generational Divide," Goodhire, published November 9, 2021. https://www.goodhire.com/resources/articles/meaning-of-work-survey/#:~:text=Following%20the%20seemingly%20always%2Dhappy,finding%20less%20meaning%20and%20purpose.

I expect you will find inspiration and confirmation of your instincts within these pages.

To improve my preparedness for the social services sector, I obtained a master's degree in public administration with a concentration in association and nonprofit management. In addition, I served as an adjunct professor in this sequence for three years. As a result, I have been on the theoretical and practical sides of nonprofit management for nearly thirty years.

When I entered the nonprofit world, I found that the lessons from Betty Harragan's book, which had saved my for-profit business career, did not apply to the nonprofit world. Throughout the years, I have discovered that those who come into the social services sector steeped in the more traditional business model do not immediately enjoy working there. These people are often out of sync with the interests of the organizations, and while they are *attempting* to engage, neither side benefits from what the other is offering. They come presenting solutions that are tone deaf to the environment and too frequently off-putting or even insulting to people experienced in this sector.

This book is meant to help all parties in this situation win. In fact, I propose that this sector is all about winning—without the need for competition. In the book, I delineate Five *C*s—Care, Community, Collaboration, Can Do, and Change—to serve as your guides when operating within the social services sector and provide more useful metaphors for the work in this environment. Let's stop talking about "battlefields" at work and setting ourselves up for unnecessary conflict. I envision an emerging ecosystem where multiple systems interact in ways that enhance development and the ability to thrive. It is happening now, and you can become part of it. I finish the book with a supportive way of identifying and addressing your unique areas of development and a quiz that helps you determine if this sector is right for you.

In offering this advice, I bring to bear my three decades in the social services arena, hard-won executive savvy, and insights as a clinical psychologist trained to foster human development. My goal is to provide you with a tangible anchor of knowledge, with guidance when you need it. At my best, I view all sides of the picture with compassion and clarity and provide my insights to help widen your own view. You will find practical solutions for dealing with the challenges the social services sector presents and taking advantage of the opportunities it provides. Successful careers and deep-down, soulful fulfillment are entirely possible in the nonprofit sector, and this book can help you find them.

CHAPTER 1

Climbing without Clobbering— a New Model, a New Orientation

I've always been in the right place at the right time.
Of course, I steered myself there.

—BOB HOPE

For much of my life, my focus was on what I wanted versus what I had. I lived a roller-coaster existence, alternating between climbing higher in my chosen field and falling inwardly when those highs never reached my hopes and dreams. Each round reinforced my fear that I would never have what I really wanted. At the time, I wasn't even aware of this as a cycle—it just felt like my life. Today, I'm aware that what generated the big highs and deep lows was discounting anything short of achieving my biggest goals. Either I made it or I missed it. Those were the only two possible outcomes. It was a worldview of extremes. But I finally learned to leave that worldview behind. My viewpoint now is a "both/and." I have *both* achieved a great deal in my life, *and* there's a lot more that I want to achieve. Those two states of mind live in communion within me, allowing me to enjoy life instead of wishing or working my days away and never being satisfied.

Part of my transformation has involved redefining what success means to me and understanding how and where to achieve it. For example, I work in the social services sector because money alone does not make me feel successful or happy. I find it an incomplete measure of success—kind of like washing your hands in water without soap. Your hands get wet, not clean, because you left out the key ingredient for handwashing. My definition of success includes using my talents to make a contribution to the world that is recognized, felt, and appreciated by those I'm serving. I am looking to make a positive impact that changes the life trajectory for individuals living in underserved communities at the intergenerational level. This goal is so much bigger than me that to reach it requires much more than me; it requires working with a lot of other people dedicated to this outcome.

To succeed at this, I need to work in partnership with those individuals. Stepping over, on, or through others to advance myself has never fit into my value system. I am more inclined to want things *for* people rather than *from* them. Those were the markers that helped me know that I landed in the right sector. And I believe that understanding this landscape and how to operate within it, finding well-placed mentors, and generating your personal definition of success will help you find your best fit in this sector too—and succeed within it.

That is the purpose of this book: to help you, to mentor you (more on mentoring later), as you figure out how to navigate the unique environment that is the social services sector.

Learning to Operate in New Ways in a New Environment

Because nonprofit, social service organizations are so different from the corporate, for-profit world, you need a new model, a new orientation, for working within this environment.

When you enter this new arena of social services, you must learn to play a new way. First, throw out the ideas you've been told about work being like combat or competitive team sports. You are neither in the military nor on a sports team. Your new work environment is not a competition, and you are not at war. It is not an arena or a battlefield. It is an ecosystem. There *are* high stakes in life, and based on their actions, people *do* come out on top or remain at the bottom. However, when you're in social services, it's those on the bottom that your agency was created to serve.

My conviction about the superiority of cooperation over competition was partially formed by the work of Margaret Heffernan, author of *A Bigger Prize: How We Can Do Better than the Competition*. She says that although competition is embedded in all aspects of our daily life, it routinely backfires on us, leading to "cheating, corruption, inequality, and risk." In addition, it destroys our ability to work together. She has found that working together "fosters creativity, sparks innovation, and reinforces our social fabric."[3] To me, these benefits seem immensely better than the negative social by-products created by competition.

I started my nonprofit career as the CEO of the North Carolina Community Health Center Association. There I had the good fortune of seeing early and firsthand the power of associating, also known

---

3   Margaret Heffernan, *A Bigger Prize: How We Can Do Better than the Competition* (Public Affairs, 2014).

as "coming together." Associations derive their power by putting those in the same industry together in a united network to promote, strengthen, connect, and achieve collective wins. In this case, the association joined together all the federally qualified health centers (FQHCs) and federally assisted nonprofit primary care practices in the state. Each CEO occupied a seat on the board of directors, and we all worked together to advocate for shared needs.

Invariably, a former hospital executive would assume one of the CEO roles in this group and break ranks when it came to meeting with elected officials and presenting mutually agreed-upon talking points. Instead, they would set up an individual meeting and represent just their particular organization's needs. The needs—and the possibilities for healthcare in the state—that they outlined were limited and therefore less compelling and impactful than those presented by the whole group. The legislative meetings that included representatives from various parts of the state showcased a vision of vertical integration and partnerships that demonstrated the full value of our care model and offered a more motivating case for supporting the policies that strengthened that model. Working with the whole group, legislators could help produce an entire ecosystem of success, rather than helping only one institution.

Once you get the concept that you're no longer in a competitive environment, deprogram yourself from thinking of the boss as a figurehead to be feared or someone who must not hear the truth. There is no room for withholding bad news and hiding mistakes in the social services sector. It is not expected—or often possible—to have a solution to every problem raised. The social services sector tackles the multilayered problems of people in some form of breakdown. It is tough, time-consuming, and overwhelming work that forces those doing it to become friends with discomfort and with not knowing. To advance, you must work through discomfort and harvest the wisdom of the collective.

For every decision that needs to be made, multiple forces are at work and have to be considered. To make the right decision, you have to be able to see the world from everyone's perspective. To assess the impact of any decision or action, you have to be able to stand in the shoes of the people involved in the issue being considered. You must incorporate compassion for all the things that touch each client's life and often have to make the choice that looks beyond productivity and organizational need.

> You climb by conducting, like the concertmaster in an orchestra, or by constructing, building a platform that takes you higher along with those who are the beneficiaries.

For example, the Innocence Project works with people who are literally in a life-or-death situation. So the people who work with them *must* be compassionate. Sometimes the people you're trying to help don't seem to care, but you have to keep in mind the depth of their need and put in the effort for them anyway. If the problems were simple, you wouldn't be in the social services sector, which by definition deals with inherently difficult social issues.

If you're considering work in the social sector, you should ask yourself these questions:

- What is driving me to be here?
- Is there a match between what the organization does and my developed skills?
- Do I respect what this organization has done and see where I can advance the mission and vision?

- What biases am I carrying (such as, "Those in the social sector couldn't cut it in the business world")?

The COVID-19 pandemic, which, at this writing, is still with us, ushered in a season of tremendous shifts. People have been forced to reexamine and restructure their lives in a way that has them entering new data into old lifestyle equations and netting different solutions. This has led to a significant number of people deciding to enter, or explore entry, into the social services sector, hoping to find meaningful work, make a difference in the world, or simply do something different.

The definition of "meaningful work," can be elusive for those who have previously settled for employment that now seems meaningless or inconsequential to them. Those who embrace the simplest definition say it's being fulfilled by doing good in the world. Some think it's synonymous with purpose and look for clues in their earlier, perhaps more idealistic, younger days to help them find that purpose. Others equate meaningful work with the Japanese concept of *ikigai*, which doesn't stop at passion but requires you to seek the union of passion, vocation, profession, and mission. This is the place that includes what you love and joins it with what the world needs and folds in what you are good at—and then finishes it off by combining all this with something that pays. Ronika Lewis, engineering product management and digital transformation leader in Google Cloud at Google, described meaningful work as something that persists long after you are gone, with impact that scales exponentially, something that changes the way we think about and do things.

On the surface, it seems great that all these people from the traditional business world want to take on this kind of work. The social services sector has always suffered from a scarcity of resources that starts with not enough seasoned and savvy professionals to do what needs to be done, and now we have a bigger pipeline of committed workers looking for meaning at a time when this sector has been called upon to do even more than usual in a disrupted world.

So this is great. Until it's not. Too often, transplants from the private sector distort, disrupt, make wrong assumptions, or look down upon their new environment. Rather than leading from a newfound Zen attitude, they enter believing that they have done, or can do, things better than the people already in this world, or they become indignant when processes or principles do not align with the working situations they left behind. The social sector can only benefit from this infusion of talent and passion if these new entrants integrate into their new environment, rather than attempting to dominate in it by overlaying their old culture onto this new (to them) culture. But the fact is, the environment, the norms, and the culture in social service organizations are different for a reason.

The people who thrive in the social services setting want to get to the top, just like everybody else in the world. But being on top may mean being a subject matter expert rather than sitting at the head of the organization. The top in social services organizations has tiers that can be equally satisfying, regardless of the "level" of the people sitting in them. So how do you climb in an environment like this? In the social services sector, you climb by *conducting*, like the conductor, concertmaster, or principal in an orchestra, or by *constructing*, building a platform that takes you higher along with those who are the beneficiaries.

Symphony Nova Scotia concertmaster Renaud Lapierre defines the *conducting* role in an orchestra this way: "The role of a conductor is to unify a large group of musicians into a core sound instead of a wild bunch of different sounds surging out ..." The primary duties of the conductor are to interpret the score in a way that reflects the specific indications in that score; set the tempo; ensure correct entries by ensemble members; and shape the phrasing of the music, where appropriate.[4] This approach corresponds to effective management in a nonprofit, where you make yourself valuable by being able to work well with others and amplify their contribution.

Those on the *constructing* path move ahead in the social services sector by using their skill at assembling various pieces into a viable whole. These people gather materials such as ideas, segments of completed work, and proven best practices from those around them, and then they combine these elements into a solid organizational or functional structure—be it the whole organization or a section, program, or project within the organization. In addition, they systematically erect, repair, and fortify the framework they've helped construct, the way a building contractor builds or reshapes a home.

Both conducting and constructing are effective ways to operate in the social services sector, but what prevents you from finding your place—and might well lead to failure—is *coasting*. In the social services sector, there is never time to coast. There is always too much to do and too few hands to do it. When you begin to coast, you operate without employing your full energy and power, dragging down others and the organization. This lack of commitment and drive diminishes productivity by the organization, which in turn limits opportunity and impact for those who need it most—sometimes desperately: those who count on your organization for services or agency.

Once you decide to work in the social sector, there are ways to advance within it without climbing on or dealing harshly with those

---

4   "What Are the Roles of the Conductor, Concertmaster, and Principals?," Symphony Nova Scotia, October 2022, https://symphonynovascotia.ca/faqs/symphony-101/ what-are-the-roles-of-the-conductor-concertmaster-and-principals/.

in your path. Here are some things to keep in mind when you start working in this environment:

Avoid the tendency to walk in and share immediate assessments that spotlight all the processes that you think are being done wrong. In this sector, *why* something is being done is just as important as *what* is being done. Learn and understand the why before you presume to criticize. Decisions make more sense when you understand the context, and context takes time to really understand.

When you are forming your initial orienting questions, make sure that your motive is to understand why and how things are done and not how to convince others that your way is better. Remember that the organization you are joining achieved enough to catch your attention in the first place. Assume that the agency has not achieved its success through luck, and honor the fact that your talents are being overlayed on a foundation that the people in the existing organization built and that you will benefit from. Those who are eager to convince others of the importance of their ideas, without understanding enough about the context, waste precious resources and time. You are there for the mission first, your ego second.

Build on what is already there. For a seasoned not-for-profit agency, you are more likely to be enhancing or evolving processes and procedures, rather than starting from scratch. The social services sector operates within constraints that require more ingenuity, perseverance, and skill than the more resourced parts of the work world. If the role you have come to fill attracted you, then innovation, a successful track record, and hard work led to its creation.

There is no need to preen and try to prove that you are the best at what you do. Those who interviewed you for your job believed what you told them during the hiring process. You need to hit the ground running with a focus on contributions that keep goals and objectives moving forward. When your focus is on proving yourself, it detracts from your ability to contribute to the mission in the way that is most needed. Working in the social sector means that you have the capacity to care about something bigger than yourself—the greater good that you and your coworkers are creating in the world.

Spend time in the beginning learning about the organizational wins that you are inheriting and the trials that have failed along the way. One of the things that plagues the social services sector is new people coming on board and trying to start over or reintroduce practices that were unsuccessful or ineffective in the past. They think they have a great new idea and don't bother to investigate what was done before. Operating this way can rob the organization of the benefit of its years of experience and the lessons it has learned along the way. Do not rely on the standard new-employee orientation to explain all you need to know about an organization's history. Each department has its own areas of success and pride, so learn about the wins relevant to each role.

Don't let the difficulties of adjusting to a new culture intensify your need to glorify or hang on to your old one. If you find yourself repeatedly referencing and romanticizing how things were done at your last job, then you are stuck looking into your rearview mirror and cannot successfully navigate forward. It is proof that you have not really transitioned out of your old job. The constant refrain of "At my last job, we _____" communicates to a group of people who like things where they are that you prefer things where you were. If you make that statement too often, you will be invited to go back to where you came from. Of course you can always share your own ideas and suggestions, but apply them in a way that is respectful of and relevant for your new environment.

Bring your whole self—your skills, your knowledge, your natural talents, your experiences, and your ideas. The more you express those things, the easier it will be to find your natural place within the organization. Diversity and inclusion initiatives that demonstrate how to put into practice respect for human rights and fairness are well underway in the social services sector. This sector's culture has been a leading force for justice and equity across all levels of the workplace and in all types of industries.

Grow yourself as you grow your career, and you will find that the personal development supports a better work and home life.

Getting Help along the Way

In this book, I will teach you what I've learned from my own experiences, and what I've learned from others, about operating in this world, and that will give you a leg up as you operate within it yourself—a kind of portable mentor, if you will. However, you will most likely need to supplement this text with well-timed, live advisors, because no matter what level of competency you bring, the social sector will present challenges that you are not equipped to conquer and that this book does not anticipate. You will need a mentor to help move you off a stuck point or accelerate your progress, but to benefit from their wisdom, you must *ask* for the help or information you need.

A mentor is someone who is further down the path than you are and is therefore able to help you see beyond where you can see for yourself. It's a bonus when they have the power to

> A mentor is someone who is further down the path than you are and is therefore able to help you see beyond where you can see for yourself.

offer a break or the next level of exposure, but that is not necessarily required for success in the social services sector. In the private sector, it is common to engage with people who believe in you, offer strategic advice, and have the power to advance your career, but they fall into the category of sponsor and should not be confused with a mentor. The added level of relationship and trust with a mentor allows you to share the personal elements as well as the professional dilemmas.

April Lewis, an executive coach and best-selling author, shared with me her experience of finding a mentor:[5]

"I have invested a lot in coaches for specific support ... but I have only had one mentor. We met on LinkedIn and had a conversation where I asked him to mentor me in business. Me asking for mentoring was not the intent of the call, but after hearing how he spoke, I knew he would be able to help me. He noticed my gift and talents immediately, and when we first spoke I remember feeling like this person was going to help me get 'discovered' and position myself to coach and speak to audiences. The interesting thing is, he has never gotten me business per se, but his advice, sound guidance, and availability when I need a listening ear has been such a blessing. He helps me think at a higher and more courageous level."

---

5   Private communication.

Tips for Finding Mentors

Sometimes you're fortunate enough to have a mentor seek you out, but more often than not, you'll need to find the right person and cultivate the relationship. Here are some useful tips for how to do that:

Identify people doing the kind of things you want to do. At some point in your work, you will need to consult with someone more seasoned than you, hopefully someone whose work you admire. Because of the tight budgets and limited workforce in the social services sector, it is highly likely that this resource will not exist within your organization, so you'll need to look elsewhere: similar organizations, conferences, lectures, authors, journals, and so on.

Relentlessly connect with potential mentors through networking, visits, and calls. You will get pearls of wisdom from many different people along the way. Consider these your mentoring moments. Look anywhere that might yield good advice, and recognize that you can have more than one mentor. Once you identify potential mentors, be intentional about keeping in touch with them.

Notice who you feel a connection with. A good mentoring relationship depends on the mentor and person being mentored feeling a kinship. Be aware of what your interactions with potential mentors feel like to you. If you feel comfortable and able to be yourself, that's a good start.

Get in touch and stay in touch. As I said above, mentors rarely fall into your lap—or, more accurately, you rarely fall into theirs—so you need to take action:

- Reach out to them and show interest in their work—they need to know you're worth their time.

- Fearlessly ask for what you need—they will have neither time to nor interest in guessing how they can be helpful to you or in constructing your personal development plan.
- Ask a short list of questions—their time is precious and should be treated as such, so know what you want to ask and keep the exchanges as succinct as possible.
- Keep in touch—the responsibility for cultivating the relationship is yours in the early stages, so make sure they know you're willing to put in the work.

Jessica Hartung, author of *The Conscious Professional*, a book about working more purposefully, shared with me her experience reaching out to a potential mentor: "I've admired Frances Hesselbein [former CEO of the Girl Scouts of America] since my twenties, when I read about her in a leadership book. I did work for the Girl Scouts, but didn't feel I knew how to reach out as a peer or colleague or someone looking for mentorship. I didn't know what I wanted or how she could help me, but I did really want to be in her presence. When I got the assignment to find the right speaker for one of my clients, I reached out to her, and told her about my interest in her work, her magazine, and referenced specific concepts she shared in a recent article."[6] This worked out well for Jessica. Frances became a mentor for, and collaborator with, her. All because Jessica felt a connection and reached out.

Look for synchronicity; recognize the little signs. Be aware of little things (including informal things) that just fall into place between you and a potential mentor: the signals, signs, and nudges that indicate a good connection between you and that person. The trick is to follow your intuition and nudges as you notice them,

---

6   Private communication.

including synchronicities. For example, you might pick up a book in the airport and then find out that the author is a keynote presenter for the conference that you are flying to attend. Notice the urge to act on this synchronicity. Follow it!

This happened to me with my mentor, Pepper Dowd. I was a big YMCAer. I had attended camp on scholarship as a child and served as a fitness instructor on nights and weekends throughout my twenties and thirties. When my work as a fundraiser for UNC–Chapel Hill required me to spend half of each month in Charlotte, North Carolina, I became a frequent user of the Dowd YMCA. My affinity for and familiarity with the place quickly deepened my connection with one of its benefactors and university alumna, Pepper Dowd. She and her dear friend Mollie Faison became my valued mentors for the six years I held the job. All this happened because I paid attention to the sign on the YMCA door that I frequently entered, which deepened my connection to Pepper.

Respect their time. In any interaction with a mentor, only ask for as little of their time as you need. You will not be the only seeker of that time, so do not treat encounters as if you were their highest priority. If you can get what you need from someone else, do so. Focus your interactions with mentors on high-value conversations that make the most of your limited time together.

Look for ways to assist them. You are building a relationship, which means the benefit must flow both ways. The relationship will not last long if you take and never give. They need to feel that you're not taking advantage of them or asking too much. You can ask, "Is there any way I can be supportive of your work?" and then follow through.

Pay for mentorship initially, if necessary. It can be worthwhile to pay for a coaching session if that is the only way to gain access to a potential mentor. Or your potential mentor may offer a webinar or have a book you can buy. And don't hesitate to buy them lunch, dinner, or other treats to get time with them. In the end, you are asking them to invest in you, and there's nothing wrong with demonstrating early that you offer a return on that investment!

You can reach whatever level of success you outline for yourself. Set your mind on a clearly defined direction, cultivate people who can help you get there, and enjoy the journey!

· · ·

In the social services sector, there is no universal definition of success. Professionals in this space must define success for themselves. Achieving success may involve a level path, with horizontal moves rather than an ascending one with increasing levels of responsibility. For example, you may determine that success for you lies in affecting individuals' living standard or health or longevity, reaching new clients, enlarging an agency's market reach, achieving spiritual enlightenment—whatever is meaningful for you. What I can tell you is that the answer to the question "What is success for me?" lies deep within you, and when you find it, it will serve as a checkpoint as you decide what comes next for you.

The following action steps will support you in gaining more clarity about your personal definition of success. Once you've defined what you want your personal successes to be, you can work toward them, but without the clarity of that definition, it's hard to know where you're going and where you'll end up. Remember, the journey to your goals and dreams is filled with highs and lows, so pace yourself, practice self-care, and celebrate along the way. I have developed a set of guidelines to help you on your way to success in the social service sector. I call them the Five Cs: Care, Community, Collaboration, Can Do, and Change. In the next chapter, I lay out the first C: Care.

Action Steps

S-U-C-C-E-S-S: What Spells Success for You?

The answer is there for all of us. We can all do this. All we need to do is press pause on everything happening outside and look inside to see the best version of ourselves.

Step One: *Close your eyes and project yourself into the future living out a successful moment.*

Step Two: *Take a mental picture or journal about what you see.*
This is what success looks like for you. Notice what you are doing, what you are wearing, your location, specific things that you see around you, and how you feel.

Step Three: *Ask yourself, if only a few things were actually going to become reality, what things would I choose?*
These are your primary motivators and the vision of them will keep you moving forward when times get tough or the journey feels too long.

CHAPTER 2

Care

Nobody cares how much you know until they know how much you care.

—THEODORE ROOSEVELT

Being mission driven is essential for success in the social services sector, because if you don't care about the work you're doing and the people you are working with, you may do more harm than good. In this chapter, I will explore care in each of these areas and remind you that your care has to extend to you and your needs as well as those around you.

Care for the Work You're Doing

One of the first lessons that I learned while training to be a clinical psychologist was that you can't care more about the client and the breakdowns in their lives than they do. Said another way, you can't want more for them than they want for themselves. I was told this over and over again, because I am one of those people who, when they engage, commit fully—ten toes down, ready to go the distance to achieve the goal. For me, establishing care in clinical psychology meant we created a treatment plan, and we both did *whatever it took* to implement that plan effectively. I am like that in all aspects of my life. I take full responsibility and am totally accountable to the people, places, processes, and pains that I engage with. I believe that this level of commitment is mandatory in social services.

When I was a psychology extern in the neuropsychology department at Children's National Hospital, two people were asked each day to arrive early and set up for testing. One person was tasked with making packets of the paperwork needed for that day and making sure that the resource box had a full supply of the necessary forms and worksheets. The other person was tasked with looking at all the evaluations that were scheduled for that day and putting the test kits that would be needed to complete those evaluations in the rooms where the evaluations would take place. This included assessments for conditions such as learning disorders, autism spectrum disorder, attention deficit hyperactivity disorder, and concussions. Those evaluations encompassed four to six hours of test administration, and the setup for them took about twenty minutes.

I *always* arrived early, which often meant that I would get the process started if someone who was supposed to do it was running late. As time went on, I found myself filling in for someone else, or just pitching in on the tasks, *every* day. Eventually, one of the neuropsychologists told me that the other externs said they didn't worry about getting in on time because they knew that I would make sure the work got done. She felt this was unfair to me and wanted me to stop. I said okay and tried to let the chips fall where they may, but I just couldn't do it. I couldn't sit back and watch the system break down. In short, I'm an "owner," and I just don't know how to be a "renter." When I commit, I commit fully—I own the work, the process, and the commitment to serving.

In the social services sector, the renter-versus-owner concept comes up often. It has to do with your level of investment, with how much you care about the work. Renters participate at the transactional level. They complete their tasks, keep their heads down, and look for someone else to make improvements, generate new ideas, solve vexing problems, and speak up when the tough conversations are needed. Owners take full responsibility, without the need for a title to go along with the duties, and fully engage in the work. This means going beyond doing only what is *asked for* and instead doing whatever is *needed*.

In the social services sector, the renter-versus-owner concept comes up often. It has to do with your level of investment, with how much you care about the work.

The social services sector was formed by owners, by folks who looked at the landscape, saw a systemic or intractable problem, and set out to solve it—without looking for additional pay or praise or a promotion. This is the level of involvement that is necessary to be successful in the social services sector. You have to care about the recipients of the services, your coworkers, the processes, the consequences, and the expenditures as if you were the owner of the organization—because, in essence, in the nonprofit sector, you *do* own the organization. Nonprofits are community assets with proceeds reinvested in a mission or used to expand the scope or vision of what the organization does. So there is no single owner, and we are all able to claim a share of ownership.

The social services sector is built on expressed values. When a social services organization incorporates, it outlines the area of need that it is going to meet, and thereafter all activities must be bent toward that end. This presumes that, when you enter as an employee, you are demonstrating with your time, skills, ideas, and activities that you are invested in the cause that you joined. In all sectors of work, people track employee engagement. Engaged employees are defined as highly motivated, as committed, as champions of the organization. They are motivated to give their best. They are neither searching for nor open to another job, because they are too busy putting their all into the job they have. They praise the organization and its causes and invite others to join them in the work they're doing—because they care about it. The social sector asks for those traits and more.

But you cannot only care about your own deliverables. You must also care for the people you work with. And that's the subject we'll look at next.

Care for Your Coworkers

Caring for those you work with means that, before you act, before you decide or denounce things, you must scan for impact. This scan involves seeing from the perspective of others. You must learn to quickly inhabit the chair of every stakeholder and envision how they will be affected by what you do. From this perspective, you will be able to see potential implementation snags, knowledge gaps, and unintended consequences. It is critical to perform this scan, because where you sit—the part of the organization, the region of the country, the managerial level, etc.—will determine how you see things.

During every new staff orientation session, I first invite each new employee to become a cocreator in the life and direction of the organization. Then I engage them in an exercise to drive home the point that my ability to make the right decisions as CEO of the organization can only be improved by letting me see through their eyes, because everyone's perspective is different and none of us can see the whole.

I call on someone sitting on each of the four sides of the rectangular conference room table and ask them to describe the room based only on what they can see straight ahead in front of them—no looking left, right, or behind when providing the description. People on one side of the table describe cabinets and a minifridge; on the other side, they describe a wall of windows; at one end of the table, they describe the TV screen and the color of the wall; and, finally, on the other end of the table, they describe a display cabinet that contains awards and commendations the organization has received. This quickly demonstrates that we all see different things from our perspective.

I then take this one step further. The large conference room we meet in allows entry from two doors that also show very different perspectives. One door opens to a very limited view of the room's content because of a partial wall; the other reveals most of the room. I then demonstrate by peeking in one of the doors that, if I were a new employee told to report to "the large conference room," my ability to recognize it would be based on which of the doors I entered, which perspective I had been given. I explain that while each person's instructions about where to enter the conference room would be right, only the description that brought me in the door with the larger view of the room would avoid confusion for me.

Good decisions can only be achieved by combining the perspectives of all observers. As CEO, I have to get everyone's perspective to decide correctly—and people in all areas of the organization should be looking for those perspectives too. I find that this lesson hits home when it is delivered in this experiential way.

Unfortunately, this ability to see beyond one's own perspective isn't always applied—especially when someone feels under pressure of some sort. For example, we are routinely visited by accreditation bodies or funders who come unannounced to validate that we are following regulations and adhering to the highest standards of care. One of those periodic visitors is the Joint Commission. Joint Commission accreditation is not attempted by many primary care practices because of the cost and time required to reach the high bar of excellence that they set. My organization was an early adopter of this quality standard and has held the quality seal for nearly two decades.

During the most recent review, one of the two Joint Commission reviewers was demanding more in-depth, on-the-spot responses than the other. For one, it was sufficient for our employees to show compliance, but the other required the immediate demonstration of conceptual and applied knowledge. As a result, for day two of their three-day visit, I decided to switch the staff assigned to shadowing each reviewer so my most seasoned team was with the more demanding assessor. This meant that one of the nonclinical staff members who had to answer questions from the less demanding reviewer would no longer have a seasoned colleague available for support. This created a great deal of discomfort for this staff member, who was going through the process for the first time.

Because of this discomfort, the staff member brought over to her office someone from one of the locations that had successfully passed the review the day before. That solution made sense from the staff member who would otherwise be alone, but from every other point of view, it was flawed. From the perspective of the staff member who was summoned, the level of personal and professional disruption was profound. Relocating unexpectedly added forty minutes to her commute, disrupting child-pickup routines. In addition, her plans to catch up after the work interruptions from hosting the Joint Commission reviewers were shot. And her chance to celebrate the previous day's victory with staff at her office and decompress from the stressful process was lost.

From my point of view, this was an inefficient use of resources. The person summoned was from the part of the organization directly providing care to our patients, which is our mission. They were not intended to serve as a safety net for headquarters and its administrative work. It would have been fine for the employee who felt uncomfortable to either tell the Joint Commission reviewer "I'll get back to you on that" for anything without a ready answer or to ask the patient care staff member to be available to join the meeting remotely, if additional insight was needed. But taking up her time and paying for her travel and parking so she could attend a ninety-minute meeting *just in case* her additional knowledge was needed did not demonstrate the appropriate level of care for her in this situation.

In the social services sector, staff-member needs have to be considered equally even in high-stakes situations like this one. Disruptions for individuals and for the agency's work need to be considered in any search for solutions. No decision is simple, because the needs of the organization as a whole do not automatically trump your personal needs. This kind of accountability demands additional time and creativity. Social service–sector staffers are expected to be nimbler, to lean into new and uncomfortable situations. The first step is to achieve a broader perspective, a bird's eye view, so you are sitting above the situation. From this perspective, it is much easier to see everyone else's viewpoint and take those viewpoints into consideration.

When you are truly able to see from the viewpoint of others, you may not like the course of action that presents itself. In that moment, it is important to remember that nothing advances or grows without discomfort. The social services sector shifts continually as it reacts to the dilemmas of the day. This means that, to thrive in this environment, you have to make friends with discomfort as much as possible.

As the leader of a social services organization, what disappoints and angers me the most is when a staff member learns about something that weakens the organization and appears indifferent to it or fails to address it, usually because of discomfort. When an employee fails to treat a problem or my direction as important, when I think those things are critical, I conclude that the person doesn't care.

The social sector requires that you go beyond *saying* that you care. You have to back up your words with consistent action. Showing that coworkers and the organization matters means following up, providing advance warning, staying behind, and a thousand other actions that demonstrate that you care. It means sacrificing on behalf of something that is bigger than yourself. (For example, the clinical staff person I mentioned above may have decided *on her own* to come and offer support to a colleague and ensure that our Joint Commission accreditation remained in place.) At some point, you may be called upon to save the day for a social services–sector organization, and that means developing into a "bigger" person, someone with a broader perspective and sense of purpose. It is not possible to achieve big in this sector by living just for yourself. We ask you to come to work to make a difference—not just for pay, personal achievement, and comradery. Those are your bonuses!

Care for Yourself

To avoid burning out, the caring that you are expected to extend outwardly must also be directed inwardly, to yourself. This self-care helps both you and the organization for which you work. I find that distraction and burnout are the forces that threaten alignment with the organization's mission and derail progress. Unfortunately, the complexity, volume, and high stakes of nonprofit work lend themselves to both distraction and burnout. For this reason, self-care must be part of your plan. Those who have long, fulfilling careers in this sector engage in meaningful activities and self-care routines outside of work.

Patrick Mutch, CEO of Chase Brexton Health Care, shared his self-care activities with me.[7]

"Every day, I look for joy and positives, large or small, in my family, work, friends, and lifestyle. In terms of day-to-day living, I eat, sleep, drink, read, pray, smile, laugh, recreate, exercise, and travel in moderation. In terms of very specific personal activities outside of family, work, and friends that refresh me, I read a variety of books and exercise to online Les Mills Body Balance, which includes tai chi, yoga, and Pilates. Prior to COVID, I did Les Mills body pump at the gym for over 12 years. Now, I find that four hours a week of just stretching and breathing are fantastic for the body, mind, and soul!"

There are hundreds of practices and activities that can refresh you before and after a hard day's work and on weekends. It's important to find the ones that work for you, that enable you to keep up with the demanding pace of social services work without burning out. The following brief self-care guide provides a number of suggestions for ways to refresh and restore yourself.

---

7   Private communication.

Self-Care Guide

- **Schedule social time with your colleagues, a support network, or loved ones.** When you have chosen to devote your career to changing the trajectory of lives, sometimes you will need to get together with others to commiserate or develop coping mechanisms for managing stress.

- **Phone a friend.** If you do not have support where you are, reach out using technology to find connections that will provide that support.

- **Step into your own personal bubble.** Find ways to shut the world out for a while. This could be as simple as putting in earbuds and closing your eyes or as elaborate as spending a day at a spa.

- **Work out.** The name says it all. When you exercise, sweat, or expend excessive energy, you are providing a space to work out any stress that you may be carrying.

- **Take a nap.** I have routinely seen social service–sector employees retreat to their car during lunch and take a nap. Those who use this practice are able to rejuvenate themselves midday.

- **Find a pastime that uses different or developing skills.** If you use your mind all day, pick something that you can do with your hands. Conversely, if your work is physical, find a way to play in your mind.

- **Laugh.** Look for humor all around you, and invent your own where there seems to be none.

- **Join those on whose behalf you are working.** When I worked for my alma mater, a public university, we were encouraged to take some time to walk around campus and immerse ourselves in student life. I have followed that practice in every organization and every population I've served since then. A twenty-minute immersion into the world of the population your agency serves provides purpose, focus, perspective, and renewed energy.

- **Create balance.** Your life is not just about giving. Find ways to receive too. Treat yourself. You're important too!
- **Find a mentor.** You do not have to go it alone or figure out everything for yourself. Find an experienced person who can advise you, and learn from their coping strategies.
- **Recognize the symptoms of stress.** Beware of negative changes in mood, appetite, energy, and sleep, and get help if those changes escalate.

• • •

When you truly care, not just about outcomes but about the people you serve and the people you work with, it leads to increased consciousness of the second *C*: Community. I'll talk about the meaning and importance of community in the next chapter.

Action Steps

Taking a Care Inventory

Caring is defined as a continuous emotional investment in a person's well-being, displayed by a desire to take actions that will benefit that individual. It is intended to actively improve a human's condition. Functioning in the social services sector requires that you begin on a platform of care.

Step One: *Develop a habit of self-care.*
Identify four to six self-care activities. Take a few moments and add these activities to your calendar. Be sure to space them out. It is better to have consistency over volume.

Step Two: *Leverage your cares.*
You will be most fulfilled working in an area that mirrors your cares. List the things that you care about and steer your career toward those causes.

CHAPTER 3

Community

He who masters the power formed by a group of people working together has within his grasp one of the greatest powers known to man.

—IDOWU KOYENIKAN

During the pandemic, my organization, a community health center, remained open for in-person care. "Open" meant that all services were offered, and all employees, regardless of function, had to come into the office every day. Most people outside the organization, and some inside, bristled at this approach, yet to me it was non-negotiable. This was our organization's 9/11 moment, the crucible of leadership, where our patients and our community needed us more than ever, and we needed each other. We would

> All we need to do to find the answers to all the world's problems is to tap into the collective, the minds of everyone living on the planet, leaving no group out.

be the ones running in to help those who were suffering, not the ones retreating home to safety. Expressing my values through my leadership meant that there would not be a two-tiered system for our staff, where some came in and some didn't. When you belong to a community and it belongs to you, everyone is in it together. You link yourself to the plight of those around you, and together you work to make it better.

In our situation, the medical patients and social services users we serve were representative of the demographic of people who were dying at a disproportionate rate from the virus. Showing up for them was about walking our talk. We had pledged to work every day to achieve health equity, and, as a fully engaged community, we were aware that resource-poor populations already faced access barriers and health disparities that would only worsen in a time of universal distress. The stakes were high, and the response had to be mighty. And our community responded mightily. Community is the most powerful force on the planet, and we unleashed the powerful energy of our community, a collection of committed interdisciplinary staffers focused on doing our best to ensure that our neighbors would survive.

One of the ways that the social services sector clicks for me as the preferred workspace is its inclusion of all members of the community. I have always believed that we have problems in this world because we segment and discount some groups within our communities. From the age of ten, I have believed that God put the answers to every single problem that plagues us on this earth in the minds of somebody here. So all we need to do to find the answers to all the world's problems is to tap into the collective, the minds of *everyone* living on the planet, leaving no group out.

The social services sector is built on this formula, and it is executed through large and small communities that work on specific problems. People come together to form organizations to support populations in need or causes that aim to better the world. Within these organizations, individuals are grouped into teams that work on aspects of the problem or cause, and outside of the organization, communities of people attach to those entities as partners. It is a series of interrelated communities that harvest collective wisdom to launch solutions and advance causes. To excel in this sector, it's critical to become a community power broker and culture cultivator. (I'll say more about these roles in the next two sections of this chapter.)

In the private sector, you have the luxury of building a team, bringing in exactly who you want or need to round out a group, to make sure it has all the elements you require. And the people you bring in usually know how to work on a team, because they're professionally mature, exposed to how a high-functioning team interrelates, and skilled at their craft. They know what is required to succeed.

In the social services sector, you don't always get to "build" a team. You are often assembling a group of people to complete tasks or working with what you have. As a result, you have to work hard to keep people aligned with the mission, to make things work, to have things mesh, because you'll have to work with some people who are young, inexperienced, early career professionals and others who are professionally underdeveloped or suffering from impostor syndrome as they work beyond their training.

What this means is that you have to work much harder at building community and cultivating culture, and if you don't learn how to do this, the challenges may do you in. I know of a tech company executive who decided to go into the social services sector, but he didn't know how to adapt to this new environment. He didn't know how to build a community around him and cultivate a supportive culture. It was jarring for him, because he'd never worked at a place where he wasn't liked—and he wasn't liked because he was viewed as out of step, with viewpoints counter to the organization's. He was always worried about looking good rather than being good or doing good work, and there is no time for those ego plays in the social services sector.

This man had never really had to cultivate a team in the private sector; it was just there. He had worked for larger corporations where everybody had an advanced degree, and everybody knew their specific role—and where there were enough people for each of them to *do* just a specific role. So he didn't have to fill gaps or help people understand how to build capacity. In a social services organization, your community is going to be inherently incomplete. Even if it has a lot of rock stars, there aren't going to be *enough* rock stars, or some rock stars are not going to have exactly the experience they need for their roles, because there's never going to be sufficient funds to segregate the duties enough to have experts in every position. So a lot of people will be doubling up on functions.

I've been told in academic training and in workshops that all you have to do is set the culture and the culture will take care of itself. But in the social services sector, cultivating a culture is an ongoing task. Because of turnover, lack of training, and professional immaturity, the culture never gets set in concrete so that it can just run itself. It's constantly disrupted. It's like a marriage, which is actually a tiny community. You can't just get married and assume that the relationship will take care of itself. Even when you're committed to each other and you're compatible and have a basic living together system that works, you still have to work at the marriage to keep it healthy and strong. The same is true in much larger communities, including public and private work settings. As the pandemic quickly becomes endemic, workforce disruption is making the highly intentional management of culture a necessity for everyone.

The Nature of Community in the Social Services Sector

One of the more difficult things to contend with in the social services sector is the constant disruption of community, both the community of people you work with and the community of people you serve. There is often consistent turnover in social services organizations, which is an ongoing challenge. And the communities you serve also change, according to what's going on in society.

For example, the unsheltered population and how to deal with their needs was totally disrupted when the pandemic hit and the bottom fell out of the economy. This created a different landscape for organizations addressing homelessness. If you had decided you were going to provide housing by turning hotels into dormitories, you had to rethink your approach. The resources for accomplishing this just weren't there, so the whole approach was thwarted. Whatever your homelessness organization had created disappeared overnight; what had been working wasn't working anymore. So the culture you'd established to accomplish this work also had to be rethought. Community disruption is embedded in the work.

In the social services sector, communities are nested and all inclusive. Meaning, to eliminate the problems within a community, everyone must have a voice and full representation within that community. That representation should include those with the least as well as those with the most. In a 2020 *Forbes* article, Tracy Brower, a sociologist and the author of the book *The Secrets to Happiness at Work*, says that "strong communities have a significant sense of purpose. People's roles have meaning in the bigger picture of the community and each member of the group understands how their work connects to others' and adds value to the whole. As members of community, people don't just want to lay bricks, they want to build a cathedral."[8]

I like Brower's analogy about laying bricks for a cathedral. When you're in the trenches in social services work, it's like being in the hot sun, slapping down that mortar and putting on those bricks. All you can see most of the time is the brick in front of you; it's hard to keep in mind that what you're building is a cathedral, something much bigger than you. No one person can build a cathedral. You not only need a lot of people laying those bars, but you also need the people who have the larger vision, who hold everyone to the plan. Everyone contributes. Everyone's contribution is essential. Everyone leaves their personal signature on the work, the way bricklayers lay their bricks in a signature way. Cathedrals are amazing community projects, and so is the work being done in the social services sector. It may not be so outwardly grand, but it's tremendously important to society.

Social services organizations need community power brokers to function at their best. This is someone who, even without position, authority, or credentials, is able to convene internal and external stake-holders and make things happen. A culture cultivator works behind the scenes to keep the environment fertile, receptive, and ready for growth and development.

Jen Pusatere, a seasoned development director, recounts an example of community power brokers at work from her days at the Madeira School:[9]

---

8   Tracy Brower, "How to Build Community and Why It Matters So Much," *Forbes,* October 25, 2020, https://www.forbes.com/sites/tracybrower/2020/10/25/how-to-build-community-and-why-it-matters-so-much/?sh=20cbc012751b.

9   Private communication.

"There were three of us—two of us in development and one in the business office—who were all in the 23-29 age range. We assessed that there was way too much dysfunction and everyone was siloed. And we literally chipped away, went into the other siloed worlds and soon other employees starting inviting us into their worlds. We got to the point where we could convene two bickering departments, put differences aside to solve the issue at hand, or move a project forward. Once that happened it was easier to then be more inclusive and cross cutting. It got to the point where the Head would say to one of us, 'We're having X problem. Do you have any ideas?' And 9 out of 10 times she would then say 'OK. Can you go tackle this for me with the least casualties?'"

The larger community of social services organizations is composed of partnerships between communities. In the American Psychological Association brochure "Safe Affirming Fair and Encouraging (SAFE) Communities," LeRoy Reese describes how people need to partner with communities to be effective:[10]

- Understand the community's culture to include its norms and values, various leadership structures, economic conditions, etc.
- Approach the community as a partner, not an experiment that is being manipulated. [Too many people treat the social services sector like an experiment, a game—and there is little time or money for things that yield losers. You must be intentional and respectful, always remembering that you're serving real people with real needs. Drug addiction and

10   LeRoy Reese, "Safe Affirming Fair and Encouraging (SAFE) Communities," American Psychological Association, accessed July 2022, https://www.apa.org/pi/families/resources/safe-schools/communities.pdf.

mental health are good examples of areas where there is a high degree of fragility in the work and damage can be done by experimentation.]

- Be intentional about establishing relationships and earning trust by working with the community's formal and informal leadership.

- Accept that while there are experts with letters behind their names, often the most knowledgeable experts are found within the community that is the focus of the engagement. [You need to be open to good ideas from unusual sources— not necessarily the one you think is the smartest person in the room. It's the people who humble themselves and learn from the community, from those you might least expect to have valuable things to say, that are most effective.]

I would add that the most lasting effects come when you develop the community's assets and strengths with a commitment to building capacity and sustainability within the community. Everyone can contribute and needs to pull their weight. The social services community can't afford to have anyone who is not active—the cost of the loss of work that needs to be done is too high.

Brower's *Forbes* article brings to mind some additional ways for individual contributors to be an effective part of the community:

- Learn the history and wins of the organization during the onboarding period to understand the context needed to design future actions and make the biggest impact as well as make good judgments.

- Be open and welcoming. Find time to talk—share ideas, stories about your work and yourself, and invite others to share.

- Clarify your purpose and identify how what you bring to the community fits into the mission or activities of the organization.
- Figure out where you fit in the workplan and within the group. A sense of belonging brings the freedom you need to contribute from your full life experience and not just academic training or work history.
- Develop understanding and agreement with your colleagues around trust, so you all feel supported and safe.
- Foster two-way accountability, skill building, and grace around missteps.
- Jump into the unknown with your colleagues. Nothing bonds better than a shared experience. Community building is accelerated when members agree to risk, overcome conflict, and make room for diverse views.
- Cultivate an organization's culture—it's as equally important as community building.

The Nature of Culture in the Social Services Sector

When a newcomer joins an organization and commits a culture violation, it is as though time stops and word finding is disabled—the silence can be deafening. Especially when the individual is unaware. It's a shocking experience all around and a test of whether the newcomer will look for guidance and receive support to become more skilled. I had this experience during a job interview with a prospective employee. I was on a panel to hire a physician recruiter, and the recruiter we were interviewing bragged to us about his willingness to go the extra mile to get candidates. He told us that he would dress in scrubs and infiltrate physician lounges in area hospitals, pretending to be a doctor, so he could cultivate the staff physicians—the *real* doctors—and find potential defectors. He thought he was demonstrating creativity and tenacity, but the panel couldn't see past the gross cultural infringement he was describing. In our culture, we *do not* impersonate professionals, poach staff from other organizations, or use dishonest gimmicks to get a win. We felt that he was only about getting a win, not taking into account whether the potential recruit would actually be a fit with our organization. Organizational culture sets the rules for behavior, and this guy had transgressed those rules before he even got the job!

Psychologist Edgar Schein developed a model for understanding workplace culture that includes three elements: artifacts, espoused values, and shared basic assumptions. I'll describe what each of these elements means to me.

Artifacts: These are the elements of an organization that are so obvious that even an outsider can see them—environmental brand, design elements, furniture, colors, uniforms, ways of operating, etc. It's important to note that these things might be clearly visible but can be hard to interpret.

Espoused values: This is how people treat each other and approach the work. These values are usually written down and should be accepted in a formal way by a new employee during the onboarding process.

> Once you join a team, be sure to understand the organizational culture and put in the work to keep it healthy and thriving.

Shared basic assumptions: These are an organization's beliefs and actions, which are so interwoven that, like artifacts, they often go unnoticed. But they form the foundation of the culture—*what* is done and *how* it is done.

It is important to check for cultural compatibility during the interview stage when you're considering working for a social services organization. Once you join a team, be sure to understand the organizational culture and put in the work to keep it healthy and thriving. Social services agencies have moved beyond practical hiring alone and are looking for cultural fit, for cultural contributors. We want people who will elevate the culture. I call the people who do this best culture cultivators. Like community power brokers, culture cultivators can be at any level in the organization.

I've heard about some great culture cultivators during my time in the social services sector. Troi was the receptionist at the National Military Family Association (NMFA). She was hyper-focused on employee morale. To give one small example, employees needed a key card to get into the organization's suite. Often, staff members would forget the key card and need to be buzzed in by Troi—and she charged them a dollar for doing it, to help encourage them to remember their card the next time. But she would use the "fines" she collected to buy surprise pizza lunches that brought everyone together for some fun. A colleague moved Troi onto her team pretty quickly after she started at NMFA, because she was underutilized as the receptionist—but Troi still made it her job to take care of employee morale. She was a natural culture cultivator.

Jose Luis, the executive director of the Special Supplemental Nutrition Program for Women Infants and Children, is another great culture cultivator. He comes in early to open up for repair men, pops in overnight to decorate an office for a staff birthday, buys gifts throughout the year so children whom the organization sees during

Christmas week can leave with a wrapped gift. He does all this off hours, with his own resources, because he wants to ensure that the people around him feel cared for.

A workplace in the social services sector is not just an environment; it is an ecosystem. It's rooted in community and culture, in people and things being interdependent and bidirectional and reciprocal. The interdependent nature of employees, colleagues, partners, communities, regulators, funders, culture, and time creates a developmental journey for workers in this sector that is akin to the developmental journey of a child. Urie Bronfenbrenner, author of the book *Making Human Beings Human*, presents a bioecological theory of development that explains how these developmental ecosystems work:[11]

- Through exploration and adaptation, people develop an understanding of the environment and acquire skills to operate within it.
- Humans are actively engaged in development.
- Adaptation to the environment is continuous and includes relationships with other people.
- Both the environment and the person are changing simultaneously, and the resulting accommodations are mutual and reciprocal [always bidirectional].
- The environment includes a variety of settings.
- The relationship between settings impacts the accommodations and is influenced by community, society and culture.

The environments in which a human being develops are like nesting dolls or a bullseye with its surrounding circles, multiple influences that surround and shape the person. Just like in the external world, in a social services–sector work ecosystem, a person operates

---

11   Urie Bronfenbrenner, *Making Human Beings Human* (SAGE Publications, Inc., 2004).

in a system of relationships, roles, activities, and settings. The person develops as a result of the system, and the system evolves as a result of the person's development. The person changes, and the system changes, because as a person develops, their actions change, and people around them respond differently toward them. (I'll go into this in more detail in a later chapter, where I apply Bronfenbrenner's ideas about environmental ecosystems specifically to the ecosystem of the social services sector.)

To understand how you have been and are being shaped by your work, you must see the environment through the eyes of others as well as your own. This will reveal the world that is being constructed within the organization and the skills that are being acquired by the people in the community, including you. These skills will help you act effectively within the organization. The ecosystem enhances development when the person's view of the world becomes extended, validated, or differentiated—or when the person becomes motivated to act in ways that are more effective for living in the environment. Again, I return to the metaphor of a marriage. The better a person is at seeing the marriage from the partner's point of view, the more that person will be able to give to, and get from, the relationship.

If your social services–sector job is not your first job, you also need to keep in mind that you bring along with you the influence of all the other environments you've worked in. You're not a blank slate. You have a point of view. It's important to be conscious of that point of view and how it influences your actions within a new organization—and if it's your first social services sector job, it's likely to be a very different kind of organization than you're used to.

•   •   •

In his *New Yorker* essay, "The Meaning of 'Culture,'" Joshua Rothman explains that workplace culture, at its best, supports people coming together to achieve "personal, humane enrichment."[12] Wisdom lies within the community, and that community forms the social services–sector ecosystem. Within that ecosystem, collaboration is paramount, and I'll discuss the nature and importance of collaboration in the next chapter.

---

12   Joshua Rothman, "The Meaning of 'Culture,'" *The New Yorker*, December 26, 2014, https://www.newyorker.com/books/joshua-rothman/meaning-culture.

Action Steps

Become a Community Power Broker

Step One: *Take Stock of your relationships, roles, activities, and environment.*

1. Ask yourself, how am I doing in building relationships? Where are my roles defined and undefined? What activities do I complete alone or as part of a team? What is the best way to describe my environment?

2. Who makes up your personal and professional communities?

3. Who is missing—given your dreams and interests, who else would be valuable for you to know and collaborate with?

4. What is the simplest way you can find missing members to add to your network? Social media is an option, but so is asking someone out for coffee, sending something that may interest them, or reaching out through friends or your networks.

Step Two: *Know the strengths of the people who make up your work community. Connect people and projects whenever possible.*

Step Three: *Identify where your contribution fits.*
Ask yourself, "How would people describe my contributions at work and in other spaces?" If you do not like the answer(s), make adjustments.

CHAPTER 4

Collaboration

Alone we can do so little. Together we can do so much.

—HELEN KELLER

There are many books to choose from to learn the value of teamwork, the steps for effective collaboration, and the benefits of working together—*Here Comes Everybody*, *The Wisdom of Crowds*, *Group Genius*, and so on. For social services–sector professionals, they are like hymnals for the choir. We are well aware of the necessity for collaboration. Our sector tackles issues for the public good, and addressing those areas of need *requires* vision and collective effort. The bigger the vision, the more dependent it is on strong internal and external collaboration.

Achieving the desired impact cannot be done without partnership. It is through collaboration that wisdom is drawn from the community and new methods, ideas, and projects are born. Collaboration also creates an avenue for everybody within a social services organization (and sometimes people within the community it serves) to contribute and shine. Every win can be traced back to a series of big and small deposits that came from a variety of contributors coming at the issue from many angles. To be successful in this sector, you need to offer what you have with one hand and form linkages with the other. That connecting hand may need to reach for new knowledge to share or interlace with another to fortify or unify efforts.

Simply put, collaboration is working with others to create or produce an outcome, and altering the way things turn out is the mission of the social services sector. For that reason, collaboration routinely happens between, as well as within, organizations. For example, I once sponsored a project that pooled the efforts of three community-based agencies in Grand Rapids, Michigan. They shared a common challenge: the users of their services were not getting better. They knew that mental health disorders and chronic health conditions (diseases that last for a year or more and require ongoing medical treatment, such as diabetes or hypertension) often occur simultaneously, but their organizations were not treating them together. As a result, neither condition was improving. Their answer was to come together to develop an integrated chronic-care model. The collaboration included nine workgroups, and services were provided through a team-based approach. Forty-five patients were selected and assigned to each care team, which included an internist, psychiatrist, nurse, health coach, medical assistant, pharmacist, and site manager. Each member of the team provided input from their area of expertise, and each patient received one treatment plan for team execution.

This collaborative model was transformative for the patients in ways that would not have been possible if each of the organizations had been working alone. One participant had diabetes and recurrent depression. Before the initiation of this program, she had been considered a noncompliant patient by all three organizations because she refused to implement the outlined interventions. The community collaboration revealed that her poor eating habits and low mood were being fueled by her living situation. She was living in the same house with her abuser. This recurrent trauma trigger created constant stress and the need to hang on to something that she controlled—food—affecting her eating patterns and her sense of self-worth. Once the full picture was known, they were able to view her with a new level of compassion and address these core issues. The focus moved from her diet and weight to finding her new housing. Once she had a safe place to live independently, her mental and physical conditions were brought to within normal limits.

Collaboration with the Vision: Followership

Corrin Colesar, who joined my organization as a human resources generalist, received three promotions within three years, ultimately serving as administrative services director. Her rise through the ranks demonstrates how collaborating with the vision of the leaders within a social services organization can advance both your career *and* the organization. Here is how Corrin describes the experience of collaborating with CCI leaders:

> "I would not consider myself to be a person who develops others. I am someone who provides support so that others can reach their fullest potential. Maybe this is the same thing. All I know is that I worked in an environment of really hardworking people. Two women in particular, Kathleen and Dr. B., were ones who I knew from very early on that I would jump off a cliff for—not blindly, of course, but because I inherently trusted them. With the kind of cliff that they would tell you to jump off, you just

knew you would be fine. This kind of trust was something that I held so dear, and it also made me want to see the two of them succeed with our organization.

For example, when Dr. B. invested time into learning the new HRSA compliance manual, I invested time into learning it, too, and did everything I could to prepare for the HRSA audit. It made me proud of the work I had done to see that she felt fully prepared for that audit.

When Kathleen wanted to roll out Studer initiatives, I practically memorized the *Hardwiring Excellence* book and started eating, sleeping, and breathing Studer. I helped her show others that the 'Studer thing' wasn't just a phase that would go away.

I liked to be the person in their corner, making sure that they were reaching their goals. They just worked too hard and for too many hours not to succeed. And I fed them—sometimes literally. I often made sure they took time to eat something while they were caught up in their work.

In short, I don't have a big story, just a series of small situations where I felt like I was the right person at the right place to contribute under the leadership of Kathleen and Dr. B."

Corrin understood that to support the leaders' vision, she had to align herself with that vision and do her part to realize it. In order to advance, she had to be a good follower first.

In a 1998 *Harvard Business Review* article "In Praise of Followers," Carnegie Mellon University Professor Robert Kelley defined this way of working as "followership—enthusiastic, intelligent, and self-reliant participation—without star billing—in the pursuit of an organizational goal."[13] He described the four essential qualities shared by effective followers:

1. **They self-manage.** Effective followers are independent thinkers who do not need close supervision or detailed direction. They can be trusted with tasks and will proactively address needs within the bounds of their skill set and authority. They put themselves on par with the leader and see themselves on a joint adventure, offering respectful feedback even when it differs from prevailing thinking.

2. **They commit to things, such as principles, people, purpose, and organizations, beyond themselves.** Effective followers focus on organizational goals and take on extra duties upon completion of their core responsibilities to ensure that those goals are met. They are self-aware and identify when things are beyond their scope and recommend colleagues who are better suited to the task.

3. **They continuously build their skills and deploy new learning where it is needed most.** Effective collaborators develop themselves for maximum usefulness through a commitment to continuous professional and personal development.

4. **They are tenacious, trustworthy, and sincere.** Effective followers reveal personal missteps, credit contributions, and share victories.

---

13   Robert Kelley, "In Praise of Followers," *Harvard Business Review*, August 1, 2014, https://hbr.org/1988/11/in-praise-of-followers.

These traits mirror those of leaders. The difference lies in the roles they hold and the activities they engage in. In the social services sector, masterful following of the leader's vision provides a fast track to the senior leader ranks.

In summary, Kelley says, "People who are effective in the follower role have the vision to see both the forest and the trees; the social capacity to work well with others; the strength of character to flourish without heroic status; the moral and psychological balance to pursue personal and corporate goals at no cost to either; and, above all, the desire to participate in a team effort for the accomplishment of some greater common purpose."[14] This is the high road to advancement in the social services sector.

On the other hand, in his leadership seminars, Bishop T. D. Jakes teaches that staff members who *cannot* align with the leader's vision really don't belong on the team. To be a good fit, each staff member must see how their vision of the work fits under the leader's vision of it.

> **If staff members are not aligned, then each person will be operating on the basis of their own vision, with their own agenda, and that creates division within the organization.**

If staff members are not aligned, then each person will be operating on the basis of their own vision, with their own agenda, and that creates division within the organization. Two different visions cannot coexist in a high-functioning organization. Divisive team members must be removed, or the leader risks losing sight of the vision and control of the organization.

---

14   Ibid.

Nontraditional Forms of Collaboration

An often overlooked and undervalued form of collaboration is within the social services organization itself. In order to effectively move your organization's mission forward, you have to look around you at how things are being done effectively and look back at where the agency came from and understand what got it to the point where you found it. As nonprofits, social services organizations must be founded on collaboration—among the people founding it, with other organizations and often with the government. Those collaborations had to be effective for the organization to succeed, so how they were achieved should be understood and appreciated by everyone who works for the organization.

Too often, social services sector organizations lose the benefit of what they've learned over their years of operation, because new entrants reinvent the wheel or leave valuable lessons and resources behind. Take the time to look through the old files, learn the organization's history, and talk to team members about past and current initiatives and resources. If you forget this piece, you're not going to be as successful, you're not going to be as helpful, and you're not going to be as valued. It is important to remember that you are just the latest collaborator in a big, ongoing collaboration.

I realized the value of the rear view when learning about photography. Most average picture-takers look forward, frame the picture, and snap. However, talented photographers recognize that sometimes the best shot is actually behind them, that looking back can provide more depth and interest to the photograph. I tried this technique on a hike. What I saw ahead was quite beautiful, but when I took a moment to turn around and look behind me, I saw the sun hitting the landscape at a different angle, one that brought out more shades of color and deeper shadows. The image I captured by looking back was even richer than the view in front of me, yielding a more interesting photograph. So be sure to look back when you join an organization, not just ahead.

Another nontraditional collaborator I found by expanding my conception of what collaboration meant was the public. For difficult decisions, I learned to call upon the general population for their collaboration. Obviously, I can't actually consult with the masses; it would be too expensive and time consuming. So I play a mental game when considering what the decision would lead to and ask myself, "Would the community approve of what would happen if I did this?" I then test my best thinking by turning my chosen decision into a newspaper headline to see if I think it would hold up to the scrutiny of people in the community reading about it. Would they approve of it? Would it seem like a good idea to them? Would it resonate with them? Would it seem like something helpful? It's a kind of self-check, to help you be more objective about your ideas and decisions.

It also ensures that you remain accountable to your primary accountability partner. Most social services organizations get funding through government grants and tax breaks—not to mention direct donations from individuals—making the public the largest payer for what your organization does in the world. It's an accountability concept, because at the end of the day, you're doing what you're doing for them, for society as a whole. They're the ultimate stakeholders. And they're the ultimate place where you're accountable. So collaborating with them in this imaginative way can be valuable.

Collaboration Currency: Communication

In the social sector, collaborations happen not only up but also down, sideways, and backward. At the team level, collaboration is a combination of distribution of tasks and discourse among those performing the tasks. If there are too many tasks or if particular tasks would be too demanding for one person or agency to handle, they need to be distributed as fairly as possible among team members. Team-member value is judged by whether they are making the workload heavier or lighter for the team. Frequent, clear communication is required to make this all work. Communication is the currency of effective collaboration.

Communication does not always occur naturally or come easily, even among people who are close personally or work closely together, but it can be learned. To best support team collaboration, any communication should be

- **easily understood**, using clear language and concepts;
- **succinct**, conveying the message using as few words as possible;
- **well timed**, because collaborators need information in time to participate at the top of their contribution level—too often, people hear about a project too late, and it limits their involvement or impacts planned activities; and
- **complete**, because full information ensures that partners will understand context and know the situation in detail.

Those receiving information must confirm with the communicator that they understand the communication before proceeding with their portion of the work, because in the social services sector, there is not enough time or resources to go off in the wrong direction. Once agreements are validated, two sides of accountability are formed. On one side is the person holding the other accountable. On the other side is the person trying to understand their accountabilities. If this loop is functioning effectively, both parties have shared goals and a clear sense of the consequences for doing things right or wrong.

I see starting the workday as an example of team collaboration with dual accountability. Once, in my organization, staff members started arriving later and later to work, which resulted in them missing important announcements during the morning huddle, information that was important to the team effort. As a result, senior leaders throughout the organization began taking attendance at the huddles and holding staff members accountable for tardiness. Several staff members were outraged at being tracked in this way, but for me it was less about following the rules and more about meeting a requirement for being part of the team and being an effective collaborator.

My reason for supporting these efforts for an on-time arrival were simple:

1. The organization's hours of operation had not changed since any of these staff members had applied for a job with us, were selected for and accepted the job, and were onboarded as members of the team.
2. Our business hours were a promise made to the users of our services, which those users relied on.
3. Failing to come to work on time to deliver on that promise was an outcome that warranted consequences.

I will note that a few staff members had external challenges that impacted their ability to control their morning schedules, but most staff members were merely refusing to be told what to do, to be "controlled." However, the point was not control but effective collaboration, which requires everyone to be able to give their input and have the same information at the start of the work day.

My response to some staff members' resistance was to explain the *why* behind the strict enforcement of timeliness and to lay out the choices. On one hand, the organization could decide to have a different set of rules based on position and location, or it could seek the board of directors' approval to change the hours of operation, or it could enforce the existing personnel policies. On the other hand, staff members could decide to adhere to the time and attendance policies, request approval for an alternate work schedule, or find a place of work where the hours better matched their morning rhythm. To my mind, none of the choices were right or wrong, but for collaboration within the organization to be effective, choices had to be made.

If this sounds harsh, keep in mind that the goal of collaboration is not to solve problems through compromise but to achieve synergies that lead to innovative solutions. The innovations needed to solve social services–sector problems require that the entire workforce pool its talents and move collectively in the same direction, with the same level of commitment to effective collaboration.

Collaboration: Conduit to Professional Development

Professional and personal development happen via collaboration too. For several decades, I spent the hours outside my day job coaching personal-training clients and teaching group fitness classes at the YMCA. I was highly successful at this, and the secret to my popularity with individual clients and class attendees was that I collaborated with them by forming a true partnership in our endeavor. While the path to health and wellness is well worn, I was able to work with each person collaboratively to add steps along that path that were fresh and unique, that got them excited about and committed to improving their health and wellness.

In the nonprofit, family-oriented fitness environment at the Y, there was a core group of fifteen students who came to my classes each week. We saw each other through challenging life experiences such as having a child, losing a child or another close relative, getting divorced, retiring, and so on. We began to offer each other "compassionate accountability," meaning that a member would share a desire or a plan after class, and we would commit to checking back in with that person in a loving and encouraging way. We never judged or condemned each other, but we held each other to our commitments and offered insight whenever we could.

One week, a member came to class right after learning of an abnormal test result. She was shaken and worried, because her scheduled biopsy was three weeks away, which felt like a long time to live with uncertainty about something so momentous. Five other women from the class spoke about a similar abnormal-lab-result experience. She got more information from them than she had gotten from her doctor, and she was able to formulate questions for her physician that helped put her at ease.

As a result of this experience, I came up with the idea of starting a virtual group wellness coaching practice and launched it the following year. This expanded our circle of 15 to 175 and drew members from around the globe! Working collaboratively with my individual clients and my original core group was the key to expanding my professional business, and it was working collaboratively with that much larger group of clients that made that business a success.

Urie Bronfenbrenner, whose work on human development informed my thoughts on the working of the social services sector as an ecosystem, says that we are always interacting with our environment and that these interactions are reciprocal and unique. This means that each of us brings our personal perspectives and experiences to each exchange. Our point of view and way of interpreting our surroundings are shaped by culture, experience, roles, personal taste, and ideology. The human ecosystem supports development when two people come together in collaboration. As they collaborate, there is an interplay where the views expressed by each are either adopted, which provides validation and makes them stronger, or differentiated, challenged in a way that calls them into question or dilutes them.

Workplace collaborations include all the ingredients that Bronfenbrenner identified as the building blocks for the ways humans develop from infants to adults:

- **Activities:** These are actions that are varied, meaningful and ongoing and increase in complexity. The lack of steady and often predictable resources in the social services sector results in never having enough workers to help with all the things that need to be done. This situation continuously provides people in this sector with opportunities to take up and do a variety of tasks more quickly than they could in another setting, where work is more specialized. It allows them to work closely with people who are engaging in complex tasks, observe what they do, participate in the execution of the task, learn how to complete such tasks—and eventually be allowed to carry them out independently.

- **Adaptation:** This involves recalibration to meet the changing demands of the social services–sector ecosystem. The need to adapt and change course is inherent in this sector. The problems being addressed are often long standing and deeply nuanced and will worsen without continual intervention.

New skills, thoughts, and approaches are needed and facilitate continual growth, and people who work in this sector have the opportunity to provide new ideas and ways of doing things once they really understand their organization's mission and the way it works.

- **Relationships:** An interaction with another that is either positive or negative, and the way we feel about those around us, influences our desire to remain in or a flee from an environment. Facing the challenges that these relationships present provides fertile ground for personal and professional development.

- **Transactions:** These are actions and reactions that create change in one or both of the collaborators in a work situation. The collaborative work environment of the social services sector assumes an atmosphere of mutual sharing. Each party is trying to contribute what is needed in the situation to maintain or establish smooth interpersonal dynamics and meet department goals. This results in a constant volley of action and reaction that fuels personal and professional development.

- **Power:** Influence and authority generates a status differential that shifts over time. The world of work always has power differentials. However, who holds the power in any given moment changes over time and in different situations. When a frontline staff member explains the breakdowns in a workflow to a room full of senior leaders, that staff person is moving toward equally balanced power with every word. The leaders are powerless to find a solution without the frontline staffer's knowledge of the system, and the staffer cannot execute a new way of doing things without approval from the leaders.

This interplay of power facilitates development for both the frontline team member and the senior leaders.

The fully collaborative work environments of the social services sector mirrors a developmentally rich ecosystem:

- It provides opportunities to form relationships with support, mutual benefits, and positive feelings.
- The balance of power at all levels shifts and routinely lands in a steady state.

When the work environment includes attitudes toward team members that are negative or neutral, mutual gain is low, and power is held narrowly. This limits development for everyone in the system and slows advancement for the organization.

•   •   •

Once you have true collaboration, you "Can Do" the job ahead of you, which is the next of my Five Cs and the subject of the next chapter. In the social services sector, you have to believe you can do things that sometimes seem impossible—that some people will be all too happy to tell you *are* impossible—and then you need resilience and grit to actually get those things done. You can't buy into the notion that you're beating your head against a wall in social services work. You can't be a professional problem-spotter within the organization. You have to believe you can make a difference and then do things that help make that happen.

Action Steps

Step One: *You will never be a good leader if you cannot follow.*

1. Check off the followership traits that you have fully developed.

   ☐ Independent, critical thinking
   ☐ Self-management
   ☐ The ability to agreeably disagree
   ☐ Credibility within the organization
   ☐ Acting responsibly toward the organization, the leader, colleagues, and yourself
   ☐ The ability to move between leading and following with ease

Step Two: *Strengthen your side of the collaboration equation.*

1. Ask yourself, what are the conditions that I need to be a good collaborator?
2. Reflect on your last collaboration challenge. Do you see things that you could have done differently?

CHAPTER 5

Can Do

You've done it before and you can do it now. See the positive possibilities. Redirect the substantial energy of your frustration and turn it into positive, effective, unstoppable determination.

—RALPH MARSTON

The social services sector requires you to believe that you can do anything—without a set course, road map, or model to follow. This sector takes on problems so big that they have sometimes proven to be insurmountable for some people and agencies. Many of these big problems have no known solution, but you must still work hard at trying to solve them. You need to believe that you can find the answer, or at least a part of the answer. To survive and thrive in this sector, you must cultivate the ability to look at big problems as tremendously challenging, not hopeless.

Does facing this kind of challenge energize you or cause you anxiety? My hope is that it is the former, because work in the social services sector is for the people who thrive in the face of adversity, who are comfortable with the unknown, who enjoy trying to achieve big goals. At the very least, career social services–sector professionals must be wired not to give up.

I learned not to give up when I was sixteen years old and participated in what Outward Bound now calls its Pathfinder Program. It was a three-week program that included one week of backpacking, one week of white-water rafting, and one week of rock climbing. The program also included a multiday solo experience in the wilderness, a community service project, and a "find your way back to camp with only a compass" navigational exercise.

This experience forced me to face a myriad of significant fears—heights, reptiles, large bodies of water, etc.—and to press forward despite those fears. When I wanted to pass on doing an activity or quit in the midst of one, I was either told by someone running the program or had to tell myself, "That is not an option." I was dropped off in the middle of nowhere and had to walk, climb, and bushwhack my way back to camp or remain in the wilderness alone. I quickly learned that I could do much more than I thought I could do and discovered that the person holding me back the most in life was me! I realized that I had a number of limiting self-beliefs that led me to be fearful, to underestimate my contributions, and to live a life much smaller than my abilities made possible.

After that experience, I decided to live *big*. I realized that I could overcome any difficulty and conquer any challenge that came my way. In essence, I had fine-tuned my self-confidence and my ability to successfully adapt to adverse conditions. This makes me confident that I can construct what is needed when nothing exists and empowers me to trust that just-in-time solutions will appear. This serves me well in the social services sector. I encourage you to build and tap into your own reservoir of confidence and adaptability to operate successfully in this sector.

Maintaining a Can-Do Attitude

It is important to develop the ability to persevere through tough times before you need to access that resolve at work. There are things you can do to accomplish this, to help you maintain a can-do attitude. Below are strategies adapted from the teachings of psychobiology to help you develop the ability to press forward through any obstacles:[15]

- **Confront your fears in whatever form they appear.** When you make it a practice to face your fears, you strengthen your problem-solving skills and strategic-planning proficiency. When you confront a fear, develop a plan for overcoming it and follow that plan until you've neutralized the fear.

- **Learn to manage stress.** When you regularly modulate your stress levels through stress-reducing activities, such as exercise, meditation, and finding the positive aspects in situations, you will develop your ability to regulate your mood and attitude when facing adversity.

- **Train yourself to be optimistic.** Your brain will operate more efficiently and help you make better decisions if you feed it with positive emotions. To that end, focus on what you can control, and accept the things that are out of your control. Recall your past successes, and document for yourself the paths that led you to those successes. Tell yourself that things will get better, and repeat words that make you feel better. Some people use affirmations on a daily basis to help themselves maintain a positive attitude. They look themselves in the mirror each morning and repeat a sentence such as, "I am capable of overcoming any problems I will encounter today."

---

15   Adriana Feder, Eric J. Nestler, and Dennis S. Charney, "Psychobiology and Molecular Genetics of Resilience," *Nature Reviews: Neuroscience* 10 (June 2009).

Social psychologist Amy Cuddy has even developed physical postures you can assume that will make you feel grounded and powerful and has done a TED Talk on the subject.

- **Reframe negative situations.** Take the time to review a challenging situation in your mind and try to understand it. Step back from the situation to look at it objectively. Then come up with several alternatives for handling the situation. This is empowering. For example, this approach is often necessary when monitoring progress on an initiative. One of my organization's goals is to decrease the number of low-birth-weight babies by increasing the number of patients in prenatal care, where mothers are provided with nutrition education and given easier access to healthy fruits and vegetables. Sometimes, the numbers at the end of the year do not show the desired reduction in low birth weights. But instead of focusing on that one metric, we take stock of all the things that *did* improve as a result of the program, such as fewer premature births because mothers have entered care earlier in their pregnancy, and more multiple births that logged healthy weights. The key is to find the wins within the data, which demonstrate that things *are* improving. You can do a similar thing with an individual project; if it doesn't work out perfectly, focus on what it *did* accomplish, not on how it failed.

- **Develop and maintain social connections.** When you get support from people with work experiences similar to your own, you feel heard and supported—less lonely in your struggle to handle difficult social services–sector problems. Social support builds comradery and that kinship gives you the courage to keep on trying.

- **Find purpose and meaning in your life.** Focusing on goals and beliefs that are bigger than yourself is an approach commonly used by resilient people. Keeping your eyes on the prize in nonprofit work helps keep you from getting too bogged down in the day-to-day hassles. It also helps if you find meaning and purpose in things you do outside of work—making art or doing crafts, meditating or being part of a spiritual community, mentoring someone—because those experiences will feed your spirit and help you maintain a positive attitude in the face of adversity.

Maintaining a Can-Do Culture

As part of my agency's culture, we ask our team members to adopt the attitude, "Yes, it can be done." This sets us up to provide the proper level of service to our patients and helps us support each other in our efforts. In addition, emphasizing this can-do attitude allows us to recognize immediately when people who join the staff are "professional" problem spotters or constant complainers, instead of problem solvers who will move our work forward.

> Things you do outside of work will feed your spirit and help you maintain a positive attitude in the face of adversity.

Professional problem spotters can always tell you what is wrong with how things are being done, and they're very proud of this ability—they actually expect to be rewarded for their "expert" insight. What they don't understand is that by continually pointing out what's *wrong* with the way things are being done, they de-emphasize what's being done *right*. They make the agency's environment *worse* by lowering morale and adding a new load to their already overloaded colleagues, draining those colleagues' energy when there is already plenty happening to siphon it. It is hard to build your resilience with people like that around you.

Michelle Hammond, associate vice president for the Library and Learning Commons at Goucher College, shared a story from her historical work experience about a staff member who seemed to excel at finding fault. When the team came together for brain storming sessions, to review and revise workflows within their areas, they were asked to list the issues they faced and collectively find solutions, or at least to chart next steps toward finding those solutions. Each time that he was called upon, this fault-finding staff member readily identified problems in *other* departments and seemed to see only what *everyone else* was doing wrong. He would angrily point out these failings from his perspective and try to win others over to his point of view.

By tirelessly amplifying his own opinions, this staff member put others off in the sessions and made them not want to participate. His negativity shifted the focus away from brainstorming to solve problems and onto griping about the problems, which solved nothing. The effort that he put into documenting the problems and present-ing a persuasive argument to get others to agree with him should have been directed at finding solutions to those problems and thereby advancing the mission of the department. When professional problem spotters focus on what *can't* be done or what *isn't* being done, instead of what *could* be done, they limit creative thinking and leave teams stalled amid the problems that *may* or *may not* exist. It is wise to avoid such people in your workplace as much as possible—and guard against becoming one yourself!

Chronic complainers have a similar impact, and if you want to advance, resist hanging around them or becoming one of them as well. I know someone who oversees thrift stores that provide job training and resources for people with disabilities. During regional meetings, she is quick to point out how hard she and her staff are working, implying that they are working harder than everybody else in the system. Her approach makes it difficult for staff from other sites to hear what she has to say and therefore adopt her best practices—which are actually good—because of the resentment her complaining engenders. This robs her of the ability to actually affect the system and make it better and to redistribute the workload among all the sites.

The social services sector needs people who are oriented toward continuous quality improvement, but the approach needs to be positive and forward looking rather than continually focusing on problems in the present. The idea is to get beyond those problems, to find solutions to them, to see how future circumstances might be a little better, rather than wallowing in the problems. A can-do attitude becomes essential for success in this sector.

• • •

The need for change is what created the social services sector in the first place, so change is a constant. To succeed in this continually changing world, you must be able to deal with the unknown and be comfortable with constant change. You need resilience, which enables you to persist through change, even when it's difficult. Resilience is what we'll explore in the next chapter.

Action Steps

Step One: *Maintain your can-do attitude.*
Accepting help and support from those who care about you and will listen to you will help you remain positive about your work.

List the people who offer supportive connections—your colleagues, friends, family members, civic group partners, and faith community.

Step Two: *Replace fears with a prevention plan.*
Write down the worst-case scenarios that grow out of your fears and beside each of those bad outcomes, write what you can do now to guard against it happening.

Step Three: *Nurture a positive self-view.*
Write positive messages or uplifting affirmations and find a way to have the affirmations appear regularly. (You can put them in your calendar, on a mirror or in a notebook.)

CHAPTER 6

Change

*Blessed are the flexible for they will not allow
themselves to become bent out of shape!*

—ROBERT LUDLUM

Change is the hallmark of the social services sector. Every social services–sector organization exists because something in society needed to change. In order to enjoy working in this sector and be effective in it, you must be able to live with, respond to, and even generate change at any given time.

To give an example, in 2017 the streets of Puerto Rico were deluged by wind and rain as the island was hit by category 4 storm Maria. My colleagues tell me that not just the streets but the street signs were destroyed by the storm, forcing them to locate structures by longitude and latitude coordinates. Power lines were disabled, making generators the only source of electricity for cooling medications and satellite telephones the only option for communication within and outside of the island. These conditions, combined with limited drinking water, fatalities, and flattened structures, compromised access to healthcare. And yet, despite this devastation and the changes it demanded in how to deliver healthcare, community health centers were expected to keep meeting the needs of patients.

In the Federally Qualified Health Center (FQHC) sector of health, where I work, we are required to change the way we provide medical services in response to any kind of disaster. In the aftermath of a hurricane, that means filling prescriptions, providing diabetic testing strips, and checking on the well-being of newborns out in neighborhoods when community members can't find their way to our doors. The ability to adapt to the situation, no matter how disastrous or demanding, is a foundation of organizations that work in the social services sector.

Social services organizations are often founded in response to broad societal needs for change. In 1912, women were expected to follow strict social guidelines and stay within narrowly defined groups, limiting their options and their power. In response to this, Juliette Gordon Low gathered eighteen girls in her home with the purpose of changing the way they looked at the world, fostering the belief that they could do anything they put their minds to. With presidential funding and recognition, those "Girl Scouts" launched a nation-wide and eventually global movement to emphasize in the lives of young girls qualities such as inclusion, self-reliance, love of the outdoors, and service to society.

> **The ability to adapt to the situation, no matter how disastrous or demanding, is a foundation of organizations that work in the social services sector.**

Because of the work of the Girl Scouts and other self-empowering organizations, girls are no longer held to strict paths in life.

However, there is still an achievement gap for girls and women in the areas of science, technology, engineering, and math. In response to this, today's Girl Scout programs have an increasing number of badges for achievement in these areas, along with particular programs that encourage girls to embrace and master computer science. Even this well-established, 110-year-old organization is still evolving and responding to the need for change!

Getting More Comfortable with Change

Becoming comfortable with ongoing change is an important self-management process. Continual change equates to continual motion. The following steps can ease the transition that change requires:

Be aware of timing. According to Dr. Katy Milkman, the author of *How to Change: The Science of Getting from Where You Are to Where You Want to Be*, we are wired to embrace change more readily during times that already feel like a new beginning. This can be the start of a new year, or even of a month or a week, or during a celebration that we associate with new beginnings, such as a birthday, graduation, wedding, etc. Whenever the beginning of a change is something you can control (and, admittedly, often it isn't), set those new goals, launch that pilot project, shift the way you're doing things at a time that feels like it's ripe for a fresh start. Doing this makes it easier for your mind to accept—perhaps even celebrate—the change, instead of resisting it.

Build in default behaviors. If you take choice out of the equation and achieve a change through required actions, you'll be able to make that change more quickly. For example, in order to increase staff interaction with its clients, one social services organization disabled the side door for staff entry and exit. This required staff members to enter and exit the building from the front, where the organization's clients waited for and accessed services. This forced the staff to encounter and greet their clients—and seeing staff members arriving on time to help them also amplified for clients the message that "we are all in this together." All this was achieved simply by taking away the choice of which door the staff used! Another example is that the supplemental food benefits given through the Women, Infants, and Children (WIC) program help clients change their eating habits. Participants can buy fresh, loose, prepackaged, cut or whole fruits and vegetables, but the benefit does not cover those same items if they are mixed with dips, sauces or dressings, which make them more fattening and less healthy. These exclusions free the clients from having to agonize over the choice and accelerates their shift to nutritious meals.

List barriers to change, and identify specific strategies to overcome them. This gives you a positive mindset toward change because you establish clear ways to deal with the difficulties it entails. For example, if your social services organization has to move to a new location, one of the barriers to making this change successful might be the added distance that clients must travel to get to your services. One strategy to deal with that would be finding a location on a bus route or securing grant funds to offer transportation to the new location through ride services.

Hold yourself accountable. It's easy to put the burden for achieving change on an accountability partner or on your boss. This goes back to what I said in chapter 2 about needing an owner-versus-renter mentality in the social services sector. You must act like an owner, and hold yourself accountable, by linking what you do or don't do to propel change to the *cost* of keeping things the way they are. You also need to be conscious of the consequences of a missed step in any change activity you undertake. For example, all grants that support my organization come with requirements, and I know that if

I fail to meet one of those grant requirements, ongoing funding for the organization will be put in jeopardy. Considering the seriousness of the consequences that might occur if you *don't* make a necessary change will help motivate you to embrace that change, or at least tolerate it, for the greater good.

Consult with peers who are dealing with change. Whatever change you need to make, it's likely that some other individual or organization in the social services sector has already made a similar change or is working on making that change. Talk with people from those organizations to find out what kind of problems they've run into and how they dealt with them. When you interact with peers facing similar issues, you can learn from what they've done and duplicate or adapt their tactics to make your change process successful, as well as gain encouragement from the fact that they made the change successfully.

Setting Boundaries

Because working in the social services sector requires the daily navigation of competing priorities, setting your boundaries is important. You need boundaries, structure, and order to keep yourself moving through the steps required to deal with change. Start with outlining what your responsibilities are and clarifying what tasks are not your concern. Think of this as establishing your "lane" in the race toward change. Once you establish your own boundaries, it has to become a two-way street: those around you must respect your boundaries, and you must respect theirs.

The need for firm boundary setting can be seen during periods of significant team-member change through turnover. During this period of instability, I have seen gossip flourish about people who were leaving the organization and people who were joining it. These untrue conversations are distracting and unproductive, so to change the way team members connected conversationally throughout the day, team members were asked to respect the following boundaries:

- Do not discuss personal information about other people.
- If you mention a current staff member in an email, a team message, or a text, you must copy them on the communication.
- If you speak about a staff member's personal business or work performance, that person must be part of the conversation.
- Find ways as a team to lift each other up and connect individually or in a group around our mission or goals.
- When someone comes to you with gossip, don't respond to the gossip, and quickly change the subject.

The absence of order and structure is a breeding ground for chaos. To use a very simple example, if you are trying to hand out box lunches during a community outreach session, failure to form lines, have enough people to hand out the boxes, and to note the food contents on each box could turn a good deed into a confusing, negative experience for the participants.

Making Change Effective

Whether it's individual or organizational, for change to happen with a minimum of disruption, your attitude has to be calibrated in the following ways:

- Be open to new things, and remain flexible.
- Be patient. Change does not happen instantaneously.

- Try another approach if something doesn't work, instead of deciding that the change is bad or can't happen. It may be a cliché, but it actually works in real life: "If at first you don't succeed, try, try again."
- Celebrate wins along the way toward making the change. A good short-term win that deserves celebration has three characteristics: it is visible, unambiguous, and clearly related to the change effort the individual or organization is undertaking. For example, if you were introducing a new program to educate teens about building wealth, celebratory milestones might include things such as creating a trending hashtag associated with the initiative, the opening of new saving accounts by the participants, and their attendance at the first financial education session. All the steps along the way are what build up to the change that a program wishes to make.

Lasting change requires that you go deep, not broad, in order to overcome the three obstacles that often block or destroy change initiatives: stress, isolation, and lack of resolve.

Stress. Uncertainty about the effectiveness of change and the outcomes it will produce are the biggest sources of stress during a change initiative in the social services sector. To reduce it, focus on the things that are within your control, even if it's something as simple as starting the day with your favorite beverage. Create routines that provide a soothing structure

> Lasting change requires that you go deep, not broad, in order to overcome the three obstacles that often block or destroy change initiatives: stress, isolation, and lack of resolve.

to your days and weeks as you deal with the inevitable stressors that change brings.

Isolation. It is easy to feel alone and discouraged when you are tackling problems that have gotten the best of your social services organization or the populations you serve. There will be periods where it feels like everyone is busy and behind, leaving them no time to give you and making you feel alone. Reject that message. You are not alone. Reach up, reach over, or reach down to identify *someone* for a brief connection that will help buoy you up. Go to someone you trust who is supportive, or find that person where you work who can always reframe things in a positive way. It can be as simple as striking up a conversation in the hall with someone who is also dealing with the change that's happening. Shared burdens are lighter.

Lack of Resolve. When change is new or progress toward it is slow, you will be tempted to abandon the new course. Stick with it. Reach for resilience, willpower, and resolve to stay the course.

• • •

Now that you understand the importance of the Five *C*s—Care, Community, Collaboration, Can Do, and Change—it's time to delve deeper into the landscape of the social services sector. We will explore the lay of the land, so you know how to negotiate your environment as your career progresses.

Action Steps

Step One: *Increase your comfort with change.*

Think about a change that is about to launch or needs to take place. Find the place when change is already built in and make that the start time.

Step Two: *Leverage your relationships to support your change effort.*
Identify the relationships that are most important to cultivate the change.

Step Three: *Identify short-term wins that you will celebrate along the way.*
(A good short-term win has three characteristics; it is visible, unambiguous, and clearly related to the change effort.)

CHAPTER 7

Redefining the Landscape

Development is the pathway to the future we want for all.
It offers a framework to generate economic growth, achieve social
justice, exercise environmental stewardship, and strengthen governance.

—BAN KI-MOON

The work environment in a capitalist society is often said to represent a chessboard, playing field, trading floor, or battlefield. I invite you to erase these kinds of metaphors from your mind when envisioning the social services–sector landscape. Instead, imagine a series of circles, like the rings of a tree. These circles represent an ecosystem of learning cycles, cycles that will allow you to understand the social services sector and develop the necessary skills to thrive in it.

Urie Bronfenbrenner developed the bioecological model of development to explain how human beings develop. It has since been applied in many disciplines, contexts, and environments as a way to examine and understand how people respond and act. His concepts help explain the social services ecosystem as a series of interconnected systems that allow for individual and group development.

The bioecological model says that a work setting (in this case, the social services sector) is a fertile ground for transformation:[16]

"When a person first participates in a setting, she or he is trying to understand the setting and what goes on in it, and is trying to learn what activities, relations, and roles are available and expected. If the person continues to participate in the setting, she or he normally will try to fit in, to become comfortable in it. The process of understanding a new setting and learning what is going on in it takes effort, and may be stressful. It may make a person anxious at first. As the person develops a clearer understanding of the setting and becomes more skilled in it, it becomes less stressful and perhaps even pleasant. As this happens, the person is more able to engage in the activities, relations, and roles available in the setting. The person is likely to become more productive, learn, and otherwise benefit from participating in the setting. If a person cannot understand or adapt to the setting, it remains stressful, and the person's behavior may be inappropriate. The person may 'adapt' to the setting by escaping it, or avoiding it, if possible."

Let's look at an example of someone who did not initially operate well within a social services environment and then examine how the organization responded poorly to her instead of developing her. Then we'll see an example of a situation that was handled better.

Muriel entered a small nonprofit agency that supported medical examinations of newly arrived refugees. Her job was to schedule the first two medical appointments, arrange transportation to and from

---

16   Lawrence G. Shelton, *The Bronfenbrenner Primer* (Routledge, 2018), 49.

the visit, confirm completion of the visits in the federal database, and make sure that the clinical team had all the forms and supplies needed to complete the work. In sum, her role was to provide the setup that was necessary for all the subsequent dominoes to fall. If her staging was off, delayed, or incomplete, the chain was broken, and program compliance for the refugees and payment to the agency were at risk.

Muriel came to this organization from a private office where duties were segregated in single units and no full process fell to any one person. She was not prepared for the transition to an environment where things were not so straightforward. Muriel tried being friendly and lighthearted in order to build relationships within the organization and gain support from her coworkers and partner agencies for the many steps that she had to complete. In the process, she often spoke in an "unfiltered" way about topics of personal interest unrelated to the program. This further slowed down a process that was already moving too slow, and it failed to foster an impression of competence with the community partners.

Muriel was constantly overwhelmed by the demands of navigating a heavy workload in an environment that demanded she be independent and self-directed. She used sticky notes to remind herself of all the many things she needed to do and to track what had already been done. Needless to say, with seventy-five new program entrants per week, these two-by-two-inch notes were an unreliable capture and organization system. Over time, Muriel became more and more flustered, and the program began to break down. Approximately nine months into the role, she received the following evaluation memo from her boss:

DATE:
TO:
FROM:

Re: Work Performance Evaluation

This memorandum is to document our conversation and outline next steps.

Professional Maturity and Cultural Incompetence

- Feedback has been received from our external partners that your telephone interactions demonstrate professional immaturity.
- Feedback from one agency in particular expressed concerns about your cultural competence.
- Feedback from your current supervisor sites poor communication, leave without approval, & inadequate accountability.

Workload and Compensation

- Your request to shift from salaried to hourly was denied. Furthermore, your request for consideration of a pay increase was denied.
- Context was provided to demonstrate that your workload is in line with your peers and high work volume is a feature of nonprofit employment.

Please plan to adhere to the following moving forward:

Professionalism

- Display improved time management. Report to meetings on time with a calm and composed demeanor.
  Note: You arrived for our meeting approximately 20 minutes late, appearing disheveled and flustered. Your email correspondence cited being delayed by a

call. Professionals plan ahead. In this instance the proper action would have been to (1) refrain from engaging with a caller near the time of an important meeting; (2) at the time that you realized that the conversation was going to interfere with the scheduled meeting, pause the interaction with the caller and see about re-scheduling; (3) notify the caller that you had to go but would call back to complete the conversation and arrive as scheduled to meet with your future supervisor.

- Manage your facial expressions and word choice during meetings. Use professional terms when describing situations and demonstrate critical thinking and analysis when communicating conclusions. *Note: During our meeting, your language, expressions, and reasoning were more aligned with an adolescent than an early career professional.*

- Maintain an organized and secure workspace. *Note: Papers should be arranged neatly within your workspace and HIPAA guidelines should be followed at all times. Presently your workspace is cluttered, filled with sticky notes with your tasks noted and not secure. Patient information is visible throughout your workspace when you are not present. Reminders, tasks and notes should be captured in a calendar, notebook/planner or white board.*

- Keep absences to a minimum

- Plan to attend upcoming Cultural Competence trainings.

Duties & Responsibilities

- Review and sign the attached job description

Workload and Performance

- Your workload and performance will be reviewed weekly during this period. Calendar invites have been issued to facilitate these discussions. Plan to report on your completed and upcoming tasks for the week. Come prepared with work samples (e.g., emails, reports, analysis, requests etc. ...), questions, ideas and logs.

- Prepare to transition all of your collateral work to me for redistribution. These duties will be assumed by a soon to be hired staff member. Once you prepare a close out report of past and upcoming activities and review that with me, those duties will no longer be included in your work scope.

- At the end of the evaluation period, a determination will be made whether your professionalism, work product and disposition fit the standards of this organization. You will either be invited to remain on the team, or you will be informed that you do not meet the requirements for the role.

Faced with this overwhelmingly negative review, Muriel decided to abort her connection with the social services organization, submitting the following notice at 10:15 p.m. on the same day she received the evaluation:

DATE: ▮▮▮▮▮▮▮▮▮▮
TO: ▮▮▮▮▮▮▮▮▮▮
FROM: ▮▮▮▮▮▮▮▮▮▮

Re: Resignation

Please accept this letter as formal notification that I am leaving my position effective tomorrow.

Thank you for the opportunities you have provided me during my time with the company. I am more than grateful to have had the opportunity of working with the team here.

If I can be of any assistance during this transition, please let me know.

In the social services work ecosystem, lessons often come through communication breakdowns with other people, and they are always bidirectional. In this maze of frustration, limited resources, and high volume, the communication flow can easily break down. This encounter could be described as a deer in headlights (the staff member) being plowed into by a fast-moving car (the manager). Both people involved had a lot of growing to do to properly fit into and thrive within the social services sector.

The staff member needed more support and guidance. She needed to be introduced to project- and time-management tools, organizational techniques, and professional-comportment mentoring so she could learn to operate in a more independent, organized, and productive way. She needed better collaboration with her boss and other team members to set up the project, and herself, for success. And if those self-development techniques didn't help improve Muriel's performance, she needed to be counseled out of the organization—and possibly the whole social services sector—in a more compassionate manner.

The manager needed to develop a better hiring process, one that would determine if potential employees had the training and skill required for their positions. In addition, he needed to learn to take more care with a low-performing team member, to communicate better with them about their work, and to help them develop the skills they needed. In the social services sector, support is often needed at the infrastructure level, because this is where the weight of an organization's responsibilities is supported, in order to keep the organizational structure standing. The abrupt departure of this staff member, and the months of difficulty for the organization that resulted from it, taught the leader to insert more support for staff members on the front end of projects and during the onboarding process so they would be prepared to handle the demands of their jobs.

Learning and Adapting

As it happens, this leader *did* acclimate to the way things should be handled in the social services landscape. He grew in managerial skill and later used a much more effective approach when a team member made a costly mistake and mishandled a situation.

This team member was responsible for collecting copayments as part of checking in patients for service. Throughout the course of one particular day, the money stored for bank deposit disappeared. She was convinced that the amount of the loss and lapse in securing the money would cost her her job. But the manager did not get angry and fire her. Instead, he handled the situation with respect and aplomb. Here is their final email exchange:

```
>> from:    Staff Member
>> to:      Manager
>> subject: Apology for Wednesday
_____

I would like to start off with an apology for
what transpired on Wednesday afternoon, this has
been a big lesson and an eye opener for me. I
take full responsibility and I know I should have
been more watchful. I am not making any excuses
for myself, I just never thought it could happen
to me, but I have taken away a valuable lesson
and a whole new appreciation for my job because
I thought my time was about to come to an end and
I realized how much I truly love it here and how
important my employment really is to me.
```

I am extremely grateful to you and my supervisor for your understanding and the compassion you have showed me. I could never thank you enough for it all. It also showed me that there is a trust that is placed on me daily not just by the patients but by you and everyone else that depends on me to turn in every cent I collect. I know how important trust is and it means the world to me to not break your trust or anyone else's.

I know what to never do again and my supervisor has also implemented a new protocol to prevent any further incidents from happening.

Thank you once again for trusting me and I hope you know how much I appreciate you and everything you do for us all.

>> **from:** Manager

>> **to:** Staff Member

>> **subject:** RE: Apology for Wednesday

Apology accepted. You received a tough lesson. I wish it did not have to come that way.

Please know that you are not defined by this one difficult incident, and we are fortunate to have you here. I trust that you learned this lesson well and thoroughly. I am also sure that you will continue to serve us well and do great things for the communities that we support.

Keep up the good work!

In the bioecological model of the social services–sector ecosystem, the benefit of this kind of exchange, compared to the previous example, is that both the manager and the employee are trying to make the relationship comfortable and productive. You can see the manager's evolution over time, his ability to adjust and recalibrate to accommodate a significant mistake made by one of his team members. This kind of treatment allowed the team member to grow in an environment of psychological safety and clearly led to that team member feeling more deeply committed to the organization.

A New Model: The Social-Sector Ecosystem

The social-sector ecosystem (SSE) is based on a series of concentric circles (adapted from Bronfenbrenner's bioecological theory of development) and their ripple effect. It is meant to create a safe space to learn, ask questions, grow, and contribute. Some people refer to this environment as a family or tribe. It is also an egalitarian environment where everyone owns what is intended to be a community asset. Every social services–sector employee is a worker, an owner, and, by proxy, the voice of the group or cause that everyone is working to advance.

The circles of the SSE include several subsystems:

- Microsystem
- Mesosystem
- Exosystem
- Macrosystem
- Chronosystem

Let's define what makes up each of these systems and how they shape the landscape of the social services sector.

The microsystem is your daily work experience. It is the smallest system level on which you operate at work. It includes your tasks, your span of control, and your interpersonal relationships, as well as how you engage and interact with your colleagues. These transactions are seen and interpreted from your unique worldview. From here, you will decide whether or not the workplace is a rewarding or toxic environment, or something in between. Because the attitude toward the microsystem is highly individual, two people working in the same space may define it in completely different ways.

> **Every social services–sector employee is a worker, an owner, and, by proxy, the voice of the group or cause that everyone is working to advance.**

The mesosystem is the circle where your development takes place. The competing priorities between work and home battle it out in this part of the system. It involves the interplay of all the circles in the SSE and the elements within them, based on their relationships with each other. For example, the mesosystem recognizes that, if you are tasked at work with ending the HIV epidemic, your efforts are impacted by community attitudes, by regulations about sex education in schools, by the actions of the local school board. Based on the various influences within the mesosystem, your strategies will need to be formed or reformed as needed—you'll need to be adaptable.

The exosystem is the setting where the forces that you cannot control, but are still affected by, live. They are often the developmental drivers that cause reactions in the mesosystem. They include things such as regulations, policies, workflows, and standards of behavior. This system also includes things such as school calendars, family values, and employee assistance resources. The exosystem can significantly define the lived experience at work.

The macrosystem[17] brings in how society defines the way we look at work and informs how we view the landscape we work in. Based on these views, we judge that things are either the way they should be or not. The macrosystem includes the beliefs and values that people use to explain why they do things the way they do them or why they relate to things in a certain way.

The chronosystem[18] is based on the fact that things change, evolve, or disintegrate over time. It also highlights the fact that for interactions to lead to development or change, they must occur regularly over extended periods of time.

The trick to settling well into the SSE is to understand that because of its highly developmental nature, it will often feel uncomfortable. Everything that you have learned about work will be tested by the work you do in this sector.

The SSE is relational and reciprocal. At every given moment, skills are being sharpened by the back-and-forth interplay happening each day. According to Bronfenbrenner, relationships have three major characteristics:

- Affect
- Power
- Reciprocity

---

17   Lawrence G. Shelton, *The Bronfenbrenner Primer* (Routledge, 2018).

18   Kate Daisy Bone, "The Bioecological Model: Applications in Holistic Workplace Well-Being Management," *International Journal of Workplace Health Management* 8 No. 4 (2015): 256–271.

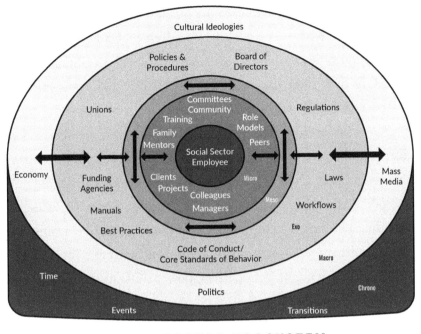

SOCIAL-SECTOR ECOSYSTEM

Note: Model Created by Author, Source: Adapted from Bone (2015)

Here is how each of these aspects of a relationship play out in the workplace.

Affect: the feelings people experience. People feel warm when a relationship is positive and cold or filled with hate when it is negative. People will stay in a system if things are mostly positive and leave it when most experiences are negative. After hearing an offensive word used while a coworker was telling a story, one listener later reported: "I was shocked and hurt by the cavalier and casual way this word was said. I did not report this right away because I needed to process my emotions around the incident and decide the best course of action." Feelings are a powerful factor in people's work experience, and because of the demanding nature of social services–sector work, people can be more emotional and more vulnerable.

Power: the strength of each person and their level of influence.
At work there is often a power differential, created either by hierarchical position or level of knowledge. While leaders usually have more authority than staff, the balance of power can shift over time and across settings. During a "course correction" conversation between a senior staff member and new employee, the staff member was so distraught because of the posture and words used by a senior colleague that she refused to talk, ran away, and ultimately left the building. At this point, the power was clearly in the hands of the senior colleague. But the next day, the employee filed a bullying charge against the senior colleague with the human resources department, immediately shifting the balance of power. These power shifts must be dealt with all the time within the workplace.

Reciprocity: the mutual sharing that happens. In an environment where reciprocity is high, information, opinions and ideas are comprehensively and freely shared. When reciprocity is low, a person may share an idea, but when they ask for information or a response in return, they might receive nothing. High reciprocity between social services–sector stakeholders sounds something like this: "We need to have a strategy for Council members who are now very aware of the important role that we play in addressing dropout rates. I have had regular conversations with individual Council members. I know from the notes shared that you all have had communications as well. We need to develop a collaborative strategy to maximize impact and make a very clear request for funding. We have made great progress over these past few years and need to keep pressing forward."

Relationships that have positive effect, power that is close to equally balanced, and high reciprocity have the most positive influence on all of us. Establishing and maintaining relationships of this kind is essential for success in the social services sector.

The Impact of Constant Change

Shelton cautions that there can be adaptation overload:[19]

"Can change be too rapid? This might be the case if a transition came before the person could adapt to the preceding one, so the person could not become comfortable and skilled in the original role or setting before the next adaptation was required. Such *adaptation* overload due to an excess of transitions might hinder construction of understanding of the ecosystem or the skills required in it. The accumulation of the stresses of change might have undesirable effects on the person both physiologically and by depressing the person's motivation to explore and maintain the ecosystem or to engage in relationships in the new setting ...

The longer the people in the system live or work or play together, the more stable the system is likely to become. The more stable and enduring the system, the more it resists change. People tend to fall into the familiar comfortable routines and habits of relating to each other."

When a person who is normally present in the workplace is absent from a team, the day looks and functions differently for the team—the ecosystem changes. The ecosystem also changes when someone new enters the workspace. In fact, when any person already in a system changes significantly, the system changes. This could be as simple as someone becoming a parent and no longer being able to work late or socialize with the group outside of work. The shake-up that comes

---

19   Lawrence G. Shelton, *The Bronfenbrenner Primer* (Routledge, 2018).

from people coming, going, and advancing becomes particularly challenging in the social services sector because of the high turnover rates, which are due to the higher volume of work and lower wages employees get compared to many of their peers in the for-profit sector.

Because of the vulnerability of the SSE, it has to be protected and nurtured. It is a developmental ecosystem, so the more you develop as an individual, the more the system develops, and the more opportunity there is for you and others. For this reason, coworkers are not just colleagues but also developmental partners. Your individual and collective interactions determine the development cycle, the development direction, and the developmental outcomes for the organization.

> **When any person already in a system changes significantly, the system changes.**

As a result, picking team members as much for mindset as for skill set is the recipe for success. When you are invited to serve on a peer interview panel, your job is to give input about the person's mindset as well as skill set. An organizational change consultant once said to me that the difference between a Nordstrom employee and McDonald's staff member is mindset. The McDonald's employee is trained to do things in a very standardized, predetermined way, whereas the Nordstrom employee needs to have the mindset of a personal shopper, taking into account the psychology and tastes of each customer they assist.

• • •

A worker's mindset and ways of acting are shaped in multiple settings, and they are constantly being reshaped by interactions within the workplace. The landscape of the workplace affects the worker's mentality, as do personality traits and past history. Each individual in the workplace sits at the center of orbiting circles or influence. The SSE model defines those circles within the social services sector, helping you understand how to achieve satisfaction within that environment, how to fit in and avoid floundering.

This book is about fitting in and finding your place, but it's also about bringing your authentic self to the table. In the next chapter, we'll look at how that's done.

Action Steps

Understanding Your Environment

To understand how you have been shaped by work, you must see the work environment from your individual perspective. This will reveal the world that you're constructing and the skills that you're acquiring. These skills will help you act effectively in the workplace.

Step One: *Embrace your place in the SSE and lean in to development.*

1. What opportunities exist for you to stretch yourself in your work?
2. How can you be the answer to a problem or need that exists in your organization? (If nothing comes to mind, what agency or community workgroup or council can you join to bring additional awareness or insight to the work that your organization does?)
3. What credentials do you have and what formal expertise can you add through certificate programs, additional degrees, or continuing education credits?

Step Two: *Manage the turbulence in your life.*

Bronfenbrenner teaches that the role that you are endeavoring to play at work must be compatible with the other settings in your life. This means that if work is in transition, you need home to be stable. Assess the status of the areas of your life, and develop interventions to ensure that your settings are set up so only one at a time will be in chaos. *(Home, Work, Volunteer or Free Time Obligations, Spiritual Life)*

CHAPTER 8

Empowerment through Equity

You get to decide where your time goes. You can either spend it moving forward, or you can spend it putting out fires. You decide. And if you don't decide, others will decide for you.

—TONY MORGAN

The power of an effective ecosystem is that everyone grows and thrives. Although every social services–sector organization was founded to address a *weakness*, your job working in this sector is to build on *strengths*. For example, I attended a talk by Reshma Saujani, a woman who, amazingly, founded a social services organization called Girls Who Code without having any software coding or high-tech experience and without ever having worked in a nonprofit organization.

After visiting high schools and seeing robotics and computer science classes filled with boys, Saujani immediately recognized the economic inequity created by the absence of women in high-tech industries. She understood that jobs in the high-tech sector paid salaries that offered a path into the middle class for women from poor backgrounds. Her answer to the gender gap, that she saw starting in high school, was to found Girls Who Code, an organization whose goal is to "inspire girls to use technology as a superpower to solve really big problems like COVID-19, cancer, and climate." From 2012 to 2022, the organization has taught 450,000 girls to code, more than half of them from underserved communities. Partially because of her efforts, the Silicon Valley pipeline has been forever transformed, and the balance of power in the high-tech industry is poised to shift.

Power gained through equity requires a shift that begins with mindset. You must believe that equity is possible and that redistributing power strengthens the whole. Bronfenbrenner defined power as the strength of each person and their influence among other people. By that definition, in my organization the most powerful people are the scheduling specialists and the patient representatives at the front desk, because we can't treat people if they don't come in. Those people control the flow of our day, and their work significantly impacts our bottom line. This view of power is very different from the view that values status and dominance. Status focuses on hierarchy and dominance on manipulation and coercion. This is not the way things operate best in the social services sector.

The social services sector is so demanding of people's time and energy and dedication that it tends to bring out weaknesses in people not prepared to deal with it. And those weaknesses can be exacerbated if they are not handled correctly. Power that is based on equity brings optimal success in this sector. It looks at what individual people have and what they are missing and tries to provide what is lacking on an individual basis, rather than assuming that everyone will benefit by receiving the same things.

The classic image in the illustration below compares equality and equity. It shows people standing on boxes to see a baseball game on the other side of a fence. In the equality illustration, each person is standing on single boxes that were assigned without consideration of individual need. As you can see, the individuals are not starting at the same level. One is standing in a lower place in front of a higher section of fence and can't see at all, and another can barely see over the fence. (Note that the one to the right has made a peephole in order to see the game, which signifies the ingenuity, workarounds, resilience, and tenacity that is evident in the social services sector.) The second illustration shows that some individuals need more boxes (understanding, guidance, support) to be equitable with the other two.

Equality vs. Equity

Your interactions with people and processes in the social services–sector ecosystem will teach you where you are standing and how many boxes you need to stand on to see over the fence—which represents the obstacles that stand in the way of your being empowered and successful. One of the things that I admire about Saujani's story is that she did not fall into the trap of comparing and contrasting ("compare and despair"), of ranking herself and knowledge against others. The fact that she had never learned to code was a nonissue in her mind, and she did not let it stop her from achieving her vision. With the right mindset, she empowered herself to be the answer to a significant generational gender problem.

The Importance of Mindset

Mark worked for a large nonprofit organization where he was well liked and valued for having great ideas and an upbeat attitude. He would often offer suggestions or ideas and lend a helping hand to make sure that projects were completed on time and according to their guidelines. Approximately one year into his tenure, things suddenly changed. He became silent during meetings and volunteered to help out less frequently. During a coaching session, he was asked what had brought on this change, and he talked about a new member of the team. "The world operates around her rhythm," he said. As he saw it, she was a person who made people better, so he didn't feel free to offer a critical analysis of anything she did. He added that she was quick witted and highly articulate, which made him feel stupid by comparison, so he had become uncomfortable speaking up.

This leads us to the first of five mindset tips I'd like to share:

Mindset Tip 1: If you're not liking how you feel,
look at your thoughts.

You have to work at not letting people get "into your head." You have to direct your focus onto your work. Don't get bogged down by comparing and contrasting yourself with others and losing sight of what *you* are contributing. It is important to remember that you are the only person who can make the contribution the way you do it. Don't let comparing and contrasting dim your light. Your gifts are equitable with everyone else's. Your organization really needs your and everybody's gifts, whether they're shiny or humble, to accomplish the work that has to be done.

Mark needed to change the direction of his thoughts and stop ranking himself against his new coworker. His feelings of being "less than" were coming from his internal monologue, not from anything anyone was saying or doing to him at work. The heavy workload, limited resources, and weight of the problems being tackled by social services agencies often leave workers stressed and a little raw. But that is where the growth edges live. Growth happens by facing difficult challenges and expanding your knowledge and skills.

Identify any gaps in what you know or can do, and bridge them. You can choose to shrink and give up in the face of such gaps, or you can choose to grow and go on to succeed. If you're feeling over-whelmed or inadequate, figure out exactly what the problem is and find ways to deal with it, which may include getting help. Ultimately, Mark was coached to help him see that his role in the organization was just as valid as what this "shiny" new coworker was contributing. Different people need more help from an organization at different times, and for the good of the whole, it's important that such help be provided.

Mindset Tip 2: All your resentments are requests that have not been made.
Stephanie came to work for a membership organization. She chose the agency because of her passion for the cause and her belief that she could focus on the industry problems and make a difference. But she became frustrated and resentful, because too often she couldn't achieve what she wanted to achieve.

Eventually, Stephanie learned that in order to meet her members' needs, she had to get help, which would enable her to focus on a few things and see them through to completion. To achieve this level of focus, she had to be good at getting help from others. Requests for help can be hard to make, because they open you up to rejection or can result in a real or perceived loss of control over a project or process. To avoid this, requests need to be made in a systematic way.

Here are a few principles to guide your communications when you make requests:

- Those you approach must have the freedom to decline a request, but most often a no means that there is a prior commitment or need the person must attend to. To avoid conflicting with the person's other concerns, issue your request in a way that speaks to those concerns and how your request can be fulfilled despite them.
- If you get a no, be aware that the person's circumstances, mood, or other obligations may prevent them from assisting at that moment—so you may not need to give up but just let some time pass before renewing your request.
- Acknowledge the interruption that the request may represent to the other person, so the person understands that you are aware of, and sensitive to, how busy they are.
- Be sure that you make a request to a specific person, with a clear statement of the action you want taken and a deadline for when you want the request fulfilled.
- Be open to your request expanding into a dialogue with the person, which will provide you with an opportunity to make your case and suggest how your request might be fulfilled.

Mindset Tip 3: Perception is not a camera; it's the filter over the camera lens.

It is not uncommon for 60 percent of the workforce within a social services organization to be in their role for the first time. For those who are entering the professional, full-time workforce for the first time, it is easy to interpret things from an incomplete viewpoint. This happened to Chet. He became so upset at the organization's decision to combine all leave into a paid-time-off bank, rather than separate buckets for sick, vacation, and personal time, that he sent his views in an indignant email to the chief operating officer and threatened to quit.

He wrote in part, "To see that all our current sick hours will be rolled over into an FML bank is heinous to say the least. This basically is a legal loophole to saying that they are gone. I did not even know what an FML account was at first and had to research the FML act and consult with my parents and coworkers. Everyone told me that I better hope I get pregnant because those 2016 accrued sick hours are gone."

Seven months later, Chet was in a serious motorcycle accident and was able to use the accumulated hours from his family medical leave (FML) bank to receive paid recovery time.

It is important to remember that the things we believe or conclude about a situation come to us after passing through a filter. Filters always change the complexion of what is being seen. Chet never imagined a day where he would need to take advantage of the Family Medical Leave Act (FMLA). But when his accident resulted in the inability to use his arms for the full three months, FMLA worked to his advantage. The angry email that he sent could have had him labeled as a complainer and troublemaker, which could have derailed his career. But the COO used the communication as an opening to broaden Chet's perspective and adjust his filters. Chet was given an opportunity to rewrite the letter to express his ideas and concerns in a way that they could evoke a reconsideration of the policy change and ways to improve employee morale.

When you have a difference of opinion with leaders or protocols, express yourself. It is okay for your first draft to be filled with passion and outrage. But *do not* send that version. Let it sit until you are less emotional, send it to a trusted colleague for a reaction, or imagine that you are receiving it rather than sending it, and decide if it is conveying the message that you intend in the best way. By taking this approach, you will learn that there is room for improvement in your ability to have a balanced perspective and that you can strengthen your ability to develop that perspective.

Mindset Tip 4: Your impact is bigger than the box you are in.
The social services sector does not work unless longtime contributors can be found in every position. Maggie has been helping people sign up for vouchers for twenty-six years. During this time, she has seen the organization change in many ways. Colleagues have moved up and out, but she is content to make a difference from the same seat. She enjoys working with families to uncover the different kinds of assistance that are available to them and ensuring that they get it. Her walls are lined with notes of thanks and pictures showing success stories from clients who leveraged county assistance to achieve a more comfortable and prosperous life. At the end of every day, she is exhausted and happy with the progress that she has made. She plans to stay in this position until she retires, because throughout the years, she has clarified for herself and others that she is fulfilled in the job she is in.

There is tremendous value to the individual and the organization in longevity. Not only does it allow you to master the work in ways that are rewarding and invaluable, but it also adds the necessary stability for the organization to thrive. A steady, contented contributor should be valued at all levels of leadership. Organizations need people who want to be in different-sized boxes. There need to be people who do not wish to supervise others, who like to be so skilled at their work that supervision is not needed, and who are fulfilled by doing what is asked without the need to alter the assignment. Such people make the best trainers and become a trusted resource for all levels. They can be counted on to be consistent, dependable keepers of the department's and organization's integrity, mission, goals, and standards.

A well-balanced and high-performing organization will usually have about 20 percent of the workforce seeking promotions; 20 percent awakening to the possibility that there can be more for them and actively building new skills; 20 percent who are new; and 40 percent who are stable, doing the work that brings them fulfillment. Never look down on what you do or the part of the organization in which you do it—or on what anybody or any other part of the organization does. Contributions are varied, and their effect is cumulative.

Mindset Tip 5: You are made smaller when you can't contribute what you have to offer.

When I first met Hazel, she was a program coordinator. During the next six years, she became a nurse and then a nurse practitioner. She was excited to move from a support role in the care team to being a provider of clinical services with her own patient panel. Unfortunately, the shift never happened for her. There was always another hoop to jump through before moving her to the new position or another delay in making it happen. It became clear to her that, if she stayed, she would be robbing herself of the advancement she had worked so hard to achieve. She could see that her agency would never see her as the clinician she had become. Instead she would always be seen as a compilation of all her past positions, with no room to progress past them. So she had to leave that agency.

In this instance, the deficiency was within the organization. The reciprocity of relationship that Bronfenbrenner espouses must exist throughout the social services ecosystem. Hazel was being diminished by evolving in place, rather than being celebrated for her accomplishments and allowed to take on a new role. The SSE needs to allow growth and evolution. When it fails to deliver on this promise to people working within it, that is proof that the system is failing and needs intervention. The choice for the individual then becomes whether to stay and participate in the overhaul or leave for another organization that is already fully functioning and healthy.

Working in the social services sector is also about living your values, but doing that does not mean that you have to eschew success and advancement. Here are five ways to live your values and still advance within the social services sector:

1. Develop a higher intention for every activity or event you're involved in.

2. Seek success and soulful fulfillment by finding work that makes you so happy and fulfilled that you lose track of time—work that also moves you in your desired direction.

3. Rather than focusing on getting yourself and people who work for you to just complete tasks, instill in yourself and them a longing for what will be achieved once the outcome is reached.

4. Show up as your authentic self, with your true thoughts, desires, and interests represented.

5. Choose to work in places where two or more of your values are already on display.

Working in the social services sector is not primarily about satisfying your ego, getting more, or becoming more important. You need to understand that this sector requires people who can work steadily and long within a smaller box. But as a professional in this sector, it *is* possible to fit in *and* stand out. Empowerment through equity happens when you fit like a puzzle piece within your organization and help fill out the picture of the organization as a whole. Sometimes your fit will make you the focal point of the action and recognition, and sometimes it will require you to keep your head down and blend in. In either position, you are adding value to the organization and can advance because of that.

• • •

After learning more about what it demands and what it offers, does it seem as if the social services sector is right for you? To help you answer that question, the final chapter of this book provides a quiz that will help you to determine whether you should engage with this sector and, if so, how best to do that.

Action Steps

We all have strengths and weaknesses. That does not mean you need to be made wrong. Stop focusing on "fixing" yourself and instead focus on evolving.

Step One: *Get out of your own way.*
Are there areas where you have held yourself back?

Step Two: *Stand in your power.*
What are the things that happen at work because you get them done? These are your power pods: list them out, and see how powerful you are!

Step Three: *Live your values.*
List each of your primary life values, and beside each, describe how your current work reflects those values.

CHAPTER 9

Personal Assessment: Finding Your Fit

But sometimes a particular purpose can be
squared with a particular career.

It may take nothing more than reexamining your career,
asking some questions, and discovering a purpose
you have overlooked in the past.

—VINCE LOMBARDI JR.

The upheaval in the working world since early 2020, mainly due to the COVID-19 pandemic, has been unprecedented. The motivation for working is changing, and that change is evident in every sector. Many people, in a quest to find deeper meaning and purpose in their work, are considering forming or joining not-for-profit organizations. I recently asked my three hundred employees why they choose to work for a nonprofit organization. The answers fell loosely into the following categories:

- They have a passion for or love of helping people in need. "When I hear about nonprofits, I feel like it's extra help for those in need. I feel that I contribute to that positive impact. I feel good knowing that I am helping people that need the help. I am grateful to see that I can help make people's lives better."
- They love working with a population that is usually grateful for the services that they receive. "It's more rewarding, and the patients are more appreciative."
- They grew up being one of those in need and want to give back. "I came from an underdeveloped country. I see how much people have struggled to get medical care. This is the population I have always wanted to work with."
- It's where people feel a sense of purpose working with others to help the underserved. "I like the environment and the people that I work with. I enjoy coming to work because it doesn't feel like work."
- They want to make a difference and have always been service oriented. "Being able to work, accomplish real results, and feel like you are making an impact is very rewarding."
- They want to benefit from federal loan repayment programs that reduce or pay off college debt in exchange for years of service in the nonprofit or public sector. "I have sacrificed a lot of time and invested a lot of money in my education. It is awesome that I can become debt-free by doing what I love for people who need it most."

Do any of these reasons resonate with you? I have found that your motivation for entering the social services sector goes a long way toward predicting whether or not you will be successful in this sector. At the end of this chapter, you will find a series of questions designed to help you determine how well you might fit as an employee in this sector. The first thing to know is that, like almost any environment you'll encounter in life, this sector is not "one size fits all." There are nonprofit organizations with budgets of $100,000 and $1,000,000,000. Some find success in this part of the working world, and others find it a clear mismatch with their talents and motivations.

There is a nice blending of skills, business orientation, and heart that can happen when a successful corporate executive makes the switch. Charlotte Min-Harris, interim president and chief executive officer at the National Service Office of Nurse-Family Partnership and Child First, was able to transition successfully based on her recognition that it takes a healthy margin to deliver on the missions that social services organizations seek to achieve:

Your motivation for entering the social services sector goes a long way toward predicting whether or not you will be successful in this sector.

"I was in the corporate sector for over twenty years and transitioned to the nonprofit world in 2009—from teaching about humanitarian work, to running an Ethiopian nonprofit, to leading development, doing grantmaking in a private foundation, to being a COO at national nonprofits. So, I've experienced the gamut and have learned much along the way. The big aha is that nonprofits *are* businesses and need "profit" to deliver the mission ... and that's okay. It's not going to the dark side. Social impact and revenue generation don't need to be mutually exclusive, because you need both to be sustainable."[20]

---

20   Private communication.

Others I've known did not find enough fulfillment to stay in the nonprofit sector. For example, Carla Wheeler, a technology, engineering, and cybersecurity executive, had this experience:

> "I provided services at a not-for-profit organization for around four years, and though prepared from a professional and service-oriented mindset, I found myself constantly defending why I was there. For some reason, the associates had difficulties understanding and accepting why I chose them over a for-profit."[21]

I have observed the suspicion of people who move over from for-profit companies that unfairly created the experience that Carla references. It typically stems from past experiences that people in nonprofits have had, where someone transferring from a for-profit company disrupted and verbally devalued their social services organization. This is something that can happen when people from for-profits can't figure out how to fit into the nonprofit organization or appear to want to change everything about it.

Leslie Graham, a nonprofit executive for nearly two decades, made a successful shift from the for-profit to the nonprofit sector supported by her familiarity through volunteer service with the nonprofit that she later joined. She has seen people who were unsuccessful due to mismatches in terms of purpose, presentation, and pay. There are different views on the purpose of a nonprofit and what constitutes its success. For some nonprofits and their boards, success is measured as growth or increased market share in the near term. They do not review their nonprofit's impact or purpose or see it as part of a larger community

21   Private communication.

service ecosystem. This market share mindset is a for-profit mindset, which can cause rifts with other nonprofit leaders in the community and therefore missed opportunities for advancing agency partnerships. Good nonprofit matches happen when converts who come over from the for-profit sector understand that their best partners may in fact be their "competitors" for the population they serve.

Presenting yourself as open and able to listen—not immediately assuming you're an expert—is essential for a transplant from the for-profit sector to succeed in the nonprofit sector. There are for-profit professionals who think nonprofit means less sophisticated, so they arrive with a know-it-all approach or the idea that they will be the one to bring that missing sophistication to the nonprofit. That angers those who have toiled hard to address the challenges the nonprofit faces and usually prevents the for-profit person from understanding the difficulties and challenges their nonprofit faces.

Leslie wonders if too many people make the switch to nonprofits in the hope of being a bigger fish in a smaller pond. To be fair, even a nonprofit professional switching to another nonprofit can be rigid and too sure of their expertise, so it isn't just a factor in the for-profit to nonprofit career change, she says. Anyone who moves within the nonprofit ecosystem needs to keep this in mind.

Experienced professionals who switch from for-profit to nonprofits later in their career thinking that an altruistic mission and purpose will make up for lower pay often find that they can't—or don't really want to—live on that lower pay rate. Then they think they can use for-profit salary negotiation tactics to improve their income, and when fixed budgets prevent this maneuvering, this kind of professional often leaves—to the detriment of the nonprofit, which could have had a longer-term employee if the for-profit professional's fit had been better assessed on the front end.

The Importance of a Good Fit

Screening for character and fit is an important step in the process of hiring in the social services sector. To that end, if you are interested in working in this sector, it is better to do your own internal review of your motivations and needs and set your sights according to what you learn about yourself. The social services sector looks for people who are focused on the needs of others rather than on personal gain.

In 2020, disability expert, and friend, Dr. George Tilson delineated the attributes of highly effective disability employment recruiters. He recently shared those attributes with me, and, amazingly, they apply perfectly to the kind of people who are well suited for working in the social services sector. These are the attributes that Dr. Tilson outlined:

1. Someone who believes in the mission and the work, with a strong personal sense of purpose. They have these traits:

    - Compassion for the people they are serving
    - High expectations for themselves and others (belief in capacity of others to achieve their goals if supports are in place)
    - Sincerity/authenticity
    - Enthusiasm/energy
    - Humor
    - Perspective
    - High self-efficacy (belief in their ability to have a positive impact)
    - Enjoyment of work
    - Satisfaction in the achievements of the people they serve
    - Expressed beliefs in the importance of the work
    - A view of needs/problems as opportunities for action
    - A "whatever it takes" philosophy

- The ability to not be easily thrown off by unexpected problems or undesired outcomes

2. Someone who takes action to get the work done and implements the mechanics of the job. They act in the following ways:

   - Implement the essential mechanics of the job
   - Display a customer-service mentality
   - Seize opportunities and take action
   - Display presence/focus as well as attention to detail
   - Understand that process and outcome must be balanced but that ultimate accountability is to measurable outcomes
   - Maintain effective strategies for managing the many facets of the work (multitasking)
   - Exhibit confidence
   - Show the ability to work creatively and efficiently to accomplish timely and useful results
   - Take risks to try out new approaches and strategies
   - Evaluate effectiveness of each approach—to determine worthiness or the need to adjust
   - Display "entrepreneurial spirit"

3. Someone who recognizes the diverse contexts in which people live their lives. They have these characteristics:

   - Recognize the context in which people live their lives, including strengths and challenges
   - Respect the roles family members play in the life of the people they serve
   - Recognize their own biases
   - Remain curious and open to new experiences
   - See the world from other perspectives

- Welcome having personal beliefs and assumptions challenged
- Find commonality with others who may be very different from themselves
- Are welcomed into others' spaces
- Are attentive to others and listen more than talk
- Enjoy learning about other cultures and traditions

4. Someone who collaborates with community members to get things done. They choose to do the following:

- Become knowledgeable about existing community resources
- Connect with others to meet diverse needs of the people they serve
- Are able to synchronize with communication styles of others
- Build personal and professional capital by introducing people to others with beneficial resources
- Are seen by other community members as a contributor, not merely a "resource seeker"
- Display balance of authority and approachability
- Demonstrate persuasiveness
- Maximize resources through collaborative efforts with others
- Demonstrate credibility and integrity

Assessing Your Fit

Attempting to enter the social services sector when another sector would be a better fit for you and attempting to do a job within the sector that is not appropriate for you will cause disruption for the agency you work with and potential heartache for you. Please take a few minutes to answer the questions on the quiz below and look deeply into what they reveal about who you are and whether you are a good fit for being employed in this sector. This will be time well spent! If you confirm that this is the right space for you and adhere to the Five *Cs* I've laid out in this book while you work in the sector, your chances of succeeding there could be much improved.

If the results indicate low fit, however, all is not lost. Consider engaging in mission-driven work in ways that allow the causes you care about to benefit from your expertise. This could be as a member of the board of directors or a consultant who discounts fees for work that is offered to social service–sector agencies. You may also decide to support social services–sector initiatives through financial contributions, as a donor or promoter. Finally, perhaps the best way to give back is as an occasional volunteer.

Social Services–Sector Entry Quiz

Whether the options before you are clear or you're still searching for your passion/purpose, the route to where you're trying to go starts from where you are right now. Take the following assessment to help determine the direction that fits for you:

Step One: *Check the characteristics that describe you.*

- ☐ Customer-service mentality
- ☐ Seizes Opportunity
- ☐ Takes Action
- ☐ Attention to Detail
- ☐ Contributor
- ☐ Persuasive
- ☐ Creative
- ☐ Balances Process & Outcome
- ☐ Multitasker

- ☐ Introspective
- ☐ Curious
- ☐ Connects with Others
- ☐ Masters Communication Styles
- ☐ Links People & Programs
- ☐ Open to New Experiences
- ☐ Takes Multiple Perspectives
- ☐ Operates with Integrity
- ☐ Holds Up to Personal Critiques

- ☐ Supportive
- ☐ Confident
- ☐ Credible
- ☐ Works Creatively
- ☐ Efficient
- ☐ Takes Risks
- ☐ Tries New Approaches & Strategies
- ☐ Evaluates Effectiveness

- ☐ Finds Commonality with Others
- ☐ Builds Rapport Quickly
- ☐ Researcher
- ☐ Listens More than Talks
- ☐ Enjoys Learning
- ☐ Honors Cultures
- ☐ Entrepreneurial Spirit

Step Two: *Circle the number that **best describes** your behavior or thinking.*

		NEVER OR RARELY	SOMETIMES	OFTEN	ALWAYS / VERY OFTEN
1.	I become anxious when things feel out of control.	0	1	2	3
2.	I prefer a set course or path with a minimum amount of uncertainty.	0	1	2	3
3.	It's okay to break the rules if I am sure I will not get caught.	0	1	2	3
4.	I believe that if I do something for you, you should do something for me in return.	0	1	2	3
5.	When I hire someone to do a job, they either have what it takes to get it done or not. It is not someone else's job to show them how to get the job done.	0	1	2	3
6.	The person with the highest job title has the most power.	0	1	2	3

7.	In work conversations, I am usually the one giving the advice rather than asking the questions.	0	1	2	3
8.	I am leaving money on the table if I do not negotiate the first salary offered.	0	1	2	3
9.	The place that I work should give me everything that I need to do my job as soon as I ask, whenever I ask.	0	1	2	3
10.	It is important to be recognized for my work.	0	1	2	3
11.	I have, since childhood, wanted to make things better for those around me.	0	1	2	3
12.	I believe that I can create a better work/life balance by working in the social services sector.	0	1	2	3
13.	Competition is inevitable between departments and within teams.	0	1	2	3
14.	I believe that the only way to advance in my career is through promotions.	0	1	2	3
15.	When things become uncomfortable, I leave or give up.	0	1	2	3
16.	I stay in contact with people from my job after I leave it.	0	1	2	3
17.	I build relationships and partnerships to get things done.	0	1	2	3

18.	When I feel frustration and stress at work, I do not complain; instead, I redirect my energy toward working my way out of the feeling.	0	1	2	3
	Totals				
	Add up the Totals				
	Results:				
	34-54	**Low Employee Fit:** This setting may be stressful for you and require extra effort. You may find your energy drained regularly and be more prone to leave.			
	20-33	**Possible Employee Fit:** This environment may require you to seek additional development. However, if you do the work, you may find fulfillment.			
	0-19	**Best Employee Fit:** This sector will most likely feel good to you. You already are wired with a compatible mindset aligned with how you approach things naturally.			

I hope the results confirmed the whispers of your heart and mind. Our internal guidance system is usually spot on in pointing us in the right direction, if we listen. Congratulations if your score revealed that you are in the right place or headed in the right direction. Remember when you internalize the number, you will have the biggest impact by engaging from the position that best fits you. Use the value to shed some light on the steps to take now. What will it be for you—employee, volunteer, donor, service discounter, or advocate?

The nonprofit sector needs your talents and your passion. There is room for everyone in some capacity. I invite you to pick your cause and your path and offer what you are best suited to give.

Connect with Dr. Bruton

Dr. Sonya Bruton on LinkedIn

YourPortableMentor@gmail.com

www.YourPortableMentor.net

About the Author

Sonya Bruton, PsyD, MPA, is the CEO and president of CCI Health Services and a licensed clinical psychologist. CCI, incorporated in 1972, is a nonprofit health system that serves 78,400 medical; dental; behavioral health; and Women, Infants, and Children (WIC) participants through twelve delivery sites throughout Montgomery and Prince George's Counties in Maryland. She has spent twenty-five years in nonprofit leadership positions and had a previous career and a successful track record in fundraising, philanthropy, strategic innovation, and community economic development. Dr. Bruton has supported nonprofit leaders as an executive coach and emerging leaders as a mentor for twenty years and has a stable of successful leaders and organizations to show for her efforts. She has also served as an adjunct professor at the graduate education level in nonprofit management. Dr. Bruton holds an undergraduate degree in journalism from the University of North Carolina at Chapel Hill, a master's degree in public administration from North Carolina State University, and a master's degree and doctorate in clinical psychology from the Chicago School of Professional Psychology at the Washington, DC, campus. She was named the 2022 John A. Gilbert Awardee, a 2022 Women Making Herstory, and a 2021 Health Care Hero.

CPSIA information can be obtained
at www.ICGtesting.com
Printed in the USA
JSHW021713050623
42744JS00001B/34